Praise for

SHE SPEAKS STORIES

"Katie Hawkins's book is a page turner! I dare you to read the first few pages and then try to put it down. It's a powerful reminder of how God transforms lives and brings beauty from ashes."

—Bob Lepine, co-host of *Family Life Today* and on-air announcer for *Truth for Life* with Alistair Begg, author of *Love Like You Mean It.*

"I am eager to share Katie Hawkins's beautiful book *She Speaks Stories* with friends, family, and colleagues who may be facing difficult times. Katie develops a personal rapport with the reader as she honestly shares her experiences, fears, and life lessons from the challenging chapters of her full life. As we follow Katie's journey of faith through her darkest times, we are encouraged to also lean into God and trust Him for our strength, answers, and direction. I highly recommend this book as a well-written, interesting, and inspiring resource for those seeking inner peace and strength."

—Donna R. Tyson, speaker, author of *The Red Bow* and founder of Infusion for Living: A Spiritual Cancer Support Group.

"God changes everything. The power of a story is one we all know well. The power of a story whose hero is Jesus is more powerful still—which is exactly what Katie Hawkins gives us through *She Speak Stories*. With a deeply personal look at the adventures of her life, we see not simply how Katie became who she is but how truly amazing God is. As a former marine and current military wife, I can find myself in Katie's words. While she takes us to hard places, we land every time in the hope of Christ. Needing some encouragement? Looking for hope? Wondering where God is? Questioning the goodness and love of God? Through *She Speaks Stories*, Katie will lead you to those answers. She'll (re)introduce you to Jesus."

—Kori Yates, director of Planting Roots,
a ministry to military women.

"Katie Hawkins is a trustworthy voice in women's lives. She communicates beautifully how to find your home in God's heart no matter where you live. If you need encouragement, you will find it in her book. It's like sitting across from a friend and finding yourself in her story."

—Jennifer Rothschild, author, founder of Fresh Grounded Faith.

"In *She Speaks Stories*, Katie Hawkins has a unique way of drawing valuable lessons from each move in her journey through life and sharing those with others in a way that gives them hope that God can redeem *every* situation in our lives for *His* good . . . *if* we allow Him to lead us even through trials and tragedies."

—Susan H. Blount, managing partner and co-founder of
the Quadrivium Group and the Blount Collective.

"Katie Hawkins is a master storyteller, weaving deep biblical truths into every page. You won't want to put the book down. Katie lives out what she teaches. I've watched her firsthand live like Jesus on the hardest of days. She's a treasure, and so is this book."

—Sharon Glasgow, pastor, Glasgow Farm Church, Proverbs 31 Ministries, Sharon Glasgow Ministries.

SHE
SPEAKS
STORIES

SHE
SPEAKS
STORIES

Finding Hope,
Help, and Healing
in a Hard World

KATIE HAWKINS

REDEMPTION
PRESS

Scripture quotations marked MSG are taken from *THE MESSAGE*, copyright © 1993, 2002, 2018 by Eugene H. Peterson. Used by permission of NavPress. Represented by Tyndale House Publishers, Inc. All rights reserved.

ISBN 13: 978-1-64645-509-6 (Paperback)
978-1-64645-507-2 (ePub)
978-1-64645-508-9 (Mobi)

LCCN: 2021919208

To my precious daughter, Molly,
and sister Denny, who lovingly
and consistently share
all the mundane stories
of everyday life with me
despite our different worldviews.

To all the Alpha team leaders and guests
I've had the privilege of sharing
faith stories with over these past years.
Nothing excites me more than
getting to hear about faith blossoming
in people's souls, and I love working
with passionate people
who share in that excitement.

CONTENTS

AUTHOR'S NOTE

A word up front about the stories I speak here. They are all negative in a sense. I write about the dark days in my life that were filled with despair or confusion or neediness. I'll warn you right up front that the negative things I've experienced will seem paltry to many of you as you deal with darkness on a level I can only imagine. But they are my trials and tribulations nonetheless. I don't tell all the delightful, happy stories that far outnumbered these bad ones. Why? The whole reason behind speaking stories of my life isn't to tell you about me, but about our Mighty God and how He helps people like me. They are about finding hope when you are in despair, help when you are desperate, and healing when you are broken. I can't showcase how He responds in times of need if I don't first explain the negative state of affairs I found myself in.

I mention this here because if you are one of the delightful people in my life who have brought me so much joy and we've had adventures together that were phenomenal, don't feel devalued that you don't appear in these stories. I could write story after story of the good times, and maybe I shall someday, but for now, these stories are about pain on some level.

Each chapter subtitle is the address of the house we lived in during that season of life. Therisa Bennett, an extremely talented artist and beautiful new friend, labored long and hard sketching each house from old pictures I'd scrounged up. I'm so grateful to her for adding a touch of class to this project!

Addressing
a Broken Heart

My daughter, Molly, was one of the first people I called to share the results of my recent breast biopsy. She is the baby of our little family of four children and the only girl. She was twenty-nine years old at the time and had chosen to live a crazy, crowded, adrenaline-filled life in New York City. From her tee-ny-tiny apartment in Manhattan, she responded to my bad news.

"Mom, I don't understand the point of praying. I've begged God these last weeks to not let you have cancer, and you do. I'm guessing He is making it clear to me that if I refuse to surrender my life to Him, He will punish me by killing you. What is the point of praying? He is going to do what He wants, and my words make no difference. I am telling you now, you can't die, because I cannot live without you. I won't stay in this world if you leave it!"

It broke my heart that my precious only daughter had such a low view of God—that she thought He was mean and punishing. It made me feel so defensive of Him because that's not what He's like at all. It also made me sad for her, because where would she find hope or help or healing for a broken heart if I were to die of this aggressive breast cancer? God had been such a rock in my own life since I'd met

Him personally in Guantánamo Bay, Cuba, the winter of 1981, before starting a life that entailed moving every year or two. I married an officer in the United States Marine Corps, Lieutenant Michael Hawkins, and his orders took us all over the country and out of it once, to Japan. It was an adventurous life, and I wouldn't trade it for anything, but it was hard. Without God pouring His love on me, I'm very sure I wouldn't have lasted. Divorce, disillusionment, and destructive addictions would have been my lot. I was somewhat of a drunk—not falling down in the gutter, but a huge party girl—when I met the Lord in a real way, and He's been healing me ever since. Oh, that Molly would understand His goodness and His unconditional love!

"Tell her! Tell her about Me," God whispered to my soul in the way He does.

"What? Hasn't she watched me all these years interacting with You, Lord? Hasn't she listened? Hasn't she heard it all? Remember the time I paid her $300 to take a course at our church so she could know You like I know You?" Truthfully, I was just forgiving her outstanding debt. I didn't fork over cold hard cash, so it felt less like an outright payment.

He instantly reminded me how ineffective that had been, as well as all my other attempts at lectures and Bible quoting and trying to convince her that a relationship with the living God beats any other human relationship hands down.

The end of my conversation with God wasn't a clear, direct voice in my outer ear, but a knowing that He had birthed in me a desire to write a book. A book would just be another medium to share what I know to be true of Him. This cancer season and my conversation with Molly at the start of it all gave me my message. "Lord, I will tell Molly, and any other dear reader who might choose to listen in, of the myriad of ways You have sent hope, help, and healing into my life these past decades."

It was the perfect season in my life to sit down and write. Normally, I like to flit around and socialize, as I abhor being alone. A cure for that restlessness came along. Not only was I going through chemotherapy treatments, but a worldwide pandemic hit all of us. Coronavirus swept through our world (and still is at the time of this writing), and we were told to stay home and keep social distance. So I had lots of time on my hands.

It made me think about some of my favorite authors who were socially isolated and used the time to write their own stories. The apostle John, banished to the island of Patmos, wrote the last book of the Bible. The apostle Paul wrote many of his fabulous letters from a Roman prison. Obviously, these men were inspired by the Holy Spirit, so they had an inarguable assignment to write, much more direct and defensible than my own. But think about Anne Frank, writing her famous diary while hiding from the Nazis in an attic. Or Lucy Maud Montgomery, author of *Anne of Green Gables*, whose childhood was exceedingly lonely, as her mother had died and her father gave her over to elderly grandparents to be raised on Prince Edward Island in Canada. She invented imaginary friends to keep the loneliness at bay, and of course, all this fed her fabulous creativity, and the world was blessed with her writings. She also lived through the Spanish flu pandemic, contracting it herself. I could go on, but my point is social isolation might lend itself to those who feel led to write.

I think the urge to write is in my blood both by nature and nurture. My dad owned and edited the local newspaper in Milton, Wisconsin, and my mom was an English teacher. Both were voracious readers, and although our house was very small, we had a huge built-in bookcase filled with books. As if those weren't enough, Mom took us to the public library, where we got "fresh" books weekly. The winters of my childhood were long and cold, and TV was allowed but kind of frowned upon as a mind-numbing activity. For great movies, we'd all congregate and watch and comment. But our time in front of the boob tube was limited. Therefore, we all read. And told each other stories.

There were six of us kids, only a year or two apart from each other. Gathering for dinner at 6:00 p.m. sharp was mandatory and always filled with lively conversation, but Thursday nights were special. We gathered early for what we called cocktail hour. It was the night the weekly newspaper was put to bed, so my dad was relaxed and able to be fully present with us. He'd share stories of the town's doings, Mom would regale us with funny stories of the knuckleheads in her English classes, and we kids would try to think up something interesting to share also. I was actually quite shy as a little girl, so my role was more listener than talker. I remember fantasizing at a young age about being an author because then I'd have time to think up stories and wouldn't have to produce one on the spot.

I remember the first story I wrote in my seventh-grade English class. My mother was the teacher, and yes, I was one of her knuckleheads. It was called "Left Hand Third Finger." We got in groups and read our stories out loud, and then the group voted for the best one. My story was picked. I was never sure if it genuinely was the best, or if my classmates wanted some points with my mom by being nice to me, but either way I got to read it out loud to the whole class. It was an extremely sappy romance, and Mom gave me some very direct editorial comments, which was embarrassing at the time. Of course they were dead on. "Don't keep repeating the title over and over within the narrative. It's redundant and stilted. People don't really talk like that, so don't write like that." I realized in hindsight what a gift Mom gave me in taking my little story seriously enough to want to help me make it better. Anyway, I'm hooked on stories but mainly reading, hearing, and verbally telling them. Writing them down is laborious! It's kind of a lonely job too. For an extrovert like me (I grew out of my shyness), a seven on the Enneagram and an ESFJ on the Meyers Briggs, it's painful.

One of my favorite authors of all time, Harper Lee, who wrote *To Kill a Mockingbird*, said this about writing:

To be a serious writer requires discipline that is iron-fisted. It's sitting down and doing it whether you think you have it in you or not. Every day. Alone. Without interruption. Contrary to what most people think, there is no glamour to writing. In fact, it's heartbreak most of the time.[1]

I don't have ironfisted discipline, but I've received so much grace and mercy from God through trials in my life and have also been the recipient of other people's beautiful stories where God steps in. My experiences with God and other people's faith stories have truly shaped me, given me courage and hope, entertained me, and enlightened me. I think it's now time to pass on a few of them. Hopefully, drops of wisdom will come your way through reading them.

One of my fervent prayers to God goes something like this:

Lord, You promise if we lack wisdom, You will give it to us freely and without reproach. You also said we need to ask without doubting, or we'll get nothing. So, Lord, I fully believe You can impart wisdom to me, and I'm in great need right now because I don't know what to do about _____.
(Fill in the blank with any number of crazy situations I've found myself in throughout the years.)

If I'm really desperate, I follow it with this plea:

Fill me with all spiritual wisdom and discernment that I might walk in a manner worthy of You, pleasing You in all respects, and bearing fruit in every good work. Lord, I don't know what to do about _____ _____, and I want to please you with my choices. I don't want to waste time doing unfruitful things, so fill me, please, with wisdom.

I'm guessing this is a somewhat universal plea no matter where or to whom we turn for some direction in decision-making.

I recently heard a TEDx talk by David G. Allan, editorial director for health and wellness at CNN. He started out by explaining human beings have been gathering wisdom for hundreds of thousands of years. It's even in our name, Homo sapiens. The word *sapiens* comes from the Latin *sapient* meaning "to be wise." Allan says the most common way we gather wisdom is through our own experiences, good or bad. This can be the least fun way. "A more consistently enjoyable one is through storytelling. And not just any stories, but the stories that speak to our human condition and that tell us what our place is in this world."[2]

Brené Brown, in her fabulous book *Rising Strong*, says, "The idea of storytelling has become ubiquitous. It's a platform for everything from creative movements to marketing strategies. But the idea that we're 'wired for story' is more than a catchy phrase. Neuroeconomist Paul Zak has found that hearing a story—a narrative with a beginning, middle, and end—causes our brains to release cortisol and oxytocin. These chemicals trigger the uniquely human abilities to connect, empathize, and make meaning. Story is literally in our DNA."[3]

So, dear reader, I'm hoping my story will help you connect with the bigger story of God at work in an ordinary life. It's my story of finding hope amid despair, help in times of trouble, and healing when bodies, souls, or relationships seem broken beyond repair—and not just my story, but the tales of others who wove their way into my own, dropping wisdom along the way.

Greenhill Circle, Milton, Wisconsin

CHAPTER 1

Pondering Thought-Jolting Conversations

I'm living a meaningless,
shallow life.
Is there hope that there's
more to life than this?

As the daughter of devout Catholics, I learned to believe in God and pray from a young age. My mom, Janet Catherine Leahy, had been educated by nuns at various Catholic schools. This did not shape her into a dainty, quiet, submissive type. She was a feisty redhead. She grew up with five brothers and knew how to hold her own in any kind of conversation. Dad asked her to write a weekly column for *The Courier,* as she had a sarcastic but charming sense of humor. She actually wrote one about how she'd like to be described if any of her children wrote a memoir[1] (included in the endnotes for you all to read so she won't haunt me if I've got it wrong).

My dad, Michael Patrick Flaherty, the oldest of ten siblings, was educated primarily through the school of hard knocks. Grandpa Flaherty was absent much of my dad's childhood. He was diagnosed with tuberculosis and therefore isolated in a sanatorium for three years. Upon return, he disappeared into the bottle for periods. So Dad took on lots of responsibilities from an early age. He worked odd jobs before and after school. He killed and plucked chickens, weeded and tended vegetables in the garden, and milked old Bessie to help put food on the table. He loved his family dearly but escaped the grinding poverty through an ROTC scholarship to Marquette University and then a hitch in the Navy during the Korean War. I had the privilege of reading a mound of letters he'd written to my mom from aboard his ship, the USS *Lenawee*. They were filled with references to his faith and the ache he had to connect with God in a real way. They also seemed to be filled with a lot of striving to do good, to be good, but messing up somewhat. Nothing flagrantly immoral or illegal, just the ordinary angst of a young man in love, wrestling with his own flawed nature—heart-wrenching stuff for me to read years after his death.

But I'm getting ahead of the story. Mom and Dad met at Tony's Bomb Shelter, a bar in San Diego. Dad was a handsome, outgoing, fun-loving sailor. Mom had vowed not to get involved with a military man, but since they both hailed from Minnesota, she agreed to go out with him. They fell in love, married, and very shortly produced six kids, one right after the other. My brother Mike came first, and his was such a difficult birth my mom told the Virgin Mary that if she helped her get through this and live to have any more children, she would name them all Mary. Three girls followed, Sheila Mary, Kathleen Mary (me), and Denise Mary. Two more boys, Tom and Jim, completed our family. By the time my brother Jim was born, we lived in Wisconsin, and my dad was a die-hard Green Bay Packer fan. Jim's middle name was Vincent, after Vince Lombardi, the famous coach who took the team to the Super Bowl. No more Marys.

We were taught to pray at meals and before bed. Not conversationally, but rotely. We didn't know about the bargaining power Mom had with the Virgin Mary till later in our lives.

"Bless us, oh Lord, for these Thy gifts, from Thy bounty, through Christ our Lord, amen" was said at mealtimes as fast as possible so we could eat.

An Our Father, a Hail Mary, and the Benediction: "As it was in the beginning, is now, and ever shall be, world without end, amen," were said at bedtimes as slowly as possible so we could get Dad or Mom to linger by our bed a bit.

And we never missed church. Well, until I hit my teen years. The family still went, but I snuck out with friends. I'd say we were going to sit together up in the choir loft or help in the "cry room" where moms with babies were to sit behind glass so they wouldn't interrupt the Mass for others, and then we'd ditch and go ride around in someone's car for an hour. I had great guilt about this, but peer pressure won the internal war, and off I'd go.

Peer pressure won in other areas also. Drinking, smoking, and shoplifting became regular activities for me in my junior high and high school days because I wanted to hang with the cool crowd, and that was the price of admission.

Actually, the shoplifting was relatively short lived. I never got caught, but it resulted in one of the first times I prayed conversationally to God. I had noticed a weird growth on my newly blooming breasts. I showed my mom, and she immediately made a doctor's appointment. Now, her appointment making might not have rattled most girls, but my mother never took our ailments very seriously. Her consistent response to most complaints was "Well, take two aspirins and go to bed."

Her response to this physical abnormality with an actual visit to the doctor freaked me out. That night, I lay in bed and bargained with God. I said something along these lines: *God, I know I've been bad. I know it's wrong to steal. I tell you what: if this lump is nothing serious and I am not ruined before I even actually start dating, I will never steal again.*

He came through. It was benign, just an abnormality. I stopped stealing. But I also stopped any meaningful conversations with God until I graduated from college. Unlike my father, I was immoral, and although I'd stopped stealing, I did other illegal things, mainly smoking pot, drinking and driving, and skipping lots of school. I often felt uneasy with the choices I was making, but not enough to stop making them.

Needless to say, I didn't think too deeply about God during those years until a thought-jolting conversation about God ensued. I'd graduated from college with a teaching degree, but jobs were very few and far between. I interviewed for one of three spots at the school where I had done my student teaching. Out of almost a thousand applicants, one of the job openings came down to me and one other person. I was sure I'd get it, but I blew the final interview.

It was August, and I was still living at home with no job and no prospects. Some mothers may have felt sorrow for one of their daughters being in that situation, but not my mom. Her motto was "We are sturdy oaks, not weeping willows." She gave me two weeks to find a job, buy a car, and get on with my life.

I remember thinking, *Are you kidding me? That's impossible! I don't even know where to start at this late date to get a teaching job.*

While I was pondering all this, the phone rang. It was the principal of a school in Beloit, Wisconsin, asking me, in a thick Irish brogue, if I'd consider coming in for an interview. I was astounded and asked how she'd even got my name and phone number. She revealed that she had called the placement office at the university I attended and asked for a list of names of newly graduated teachers.

When the placement officer read out my name, Kathleen Mary Flaherty, she said, "That's the one, thank you very much."

Sister Candice made an instant decision that, with a name like mine, I would fit right in at Our Lady of the Assumption Catholic School, run by a group of Irish nuns. I got the job, I bought a car, and I moved into an apartment with the fifth-grade teacher, all in a matter of weeks, much to my mother's relief.

This turn of events prompted me to ask my father, "Dad, do you think God directly intervenes in our lives? Because I think it's so crazy that I was in such an impossible situation and out of the blue I get a call from a nun offering me a job. Do you think that was God orchestrating that?"

His answer, after some careful thought, "No, I think God just puts us down here on earth and expects us to do our best."

This was my first pulling away mentally from someone else's opinion about God. I highly respected my dad. He was a brilliant man and a good man. But I was very confused about his answer. I thought, *Well, why does anyone go to church or pray? Ever? If God isn't really involved with us, then why do we involve ourselves with Him in any way?*

Off I went to teach reading, writing, and arithmetic—oh, and religion too.

I had absolutely no clue what I was talking about as we discussed Jesus and religion. So I made stuff up. I'll never forget the time a fourth grader asked me how communion was the actual body and blood of Jesus Christ. I thought about it, not deeply, and answered, "Well, it's not the real body and blood. It's just a symbol. I mean, look at the story of the Last Supper. Jesus had his body and blood still intact when He said, 'This is my body.' So he must've been just talking symbolically."

The boy went home and told his mom what I said. The mom called the priest, who was at my classroom door the very next day.

This was the second conversation that caused me to pull away from someone else's opinion of God. The priest told me that the absolute most important thing about our religion was believing in the transubstantiation. I said, "So believing the host is changed into real flesh and blood during Mass is more important than what Jesus Himself said the most important thing was? Didn't He say that loving God and loving others was the most important thing?"

I guess he thought I was being a smart aleck. He said, "Yes, actually it is the most important! How can you even call yourself a Catholic if you don't believe this most basic of truths? What did you think the whole Mass was about all these years you've been attending?"

Truthfully, that conversation was such a gift because it made me wonder what I actually believed. For the first time, I really wanted to stop and ponder faith and religion and God and all of it.

One of the nuns, Sister Anna, helped me get started in sorting it all out. She was so lovely—not necessarily physically beautiful, but a gorgeous spirit flowed out of her. Everybody loved her, including the seventh-grade boys who generally loved no one. She treated me like I imagined Jesus treated people. I blatantly smoked cigarettes in the teachers' lounge, and while most of the nuns exited when I lit up, she'd stay and chat with me. I came in every Monday morning with a serious hangover, wincing at loud noises. She was always gentle with me. Obviously, I wasn't the best role model for the fourth graders I was entrusted with, since I had been caught teaching heresy. Yet Sister Anna would greet me with love, invite me over to the convent where she lived, ask me about my life and really listen, and, best of all, encourage me to consider Jesus in a new way. She wanted me to understand that He was real and alive and active in our world and that He loved me. She also wanted me to be a nun. This surprisingly touched me, as she knew I was messing around with the lead guitar player in a rock band at the time. She knew my habits, my sins, and my ignorance, yet she had a confidence that God loved me and wanted me to know Him.

She gave me a Bible. I tried to read it for Lent instead of giving up chocolate, my usual Lenten sacrifice, as I didn't really like chocolate all that much. I got through Genesis and Exodus but came to a dead stop when I hit Numbers. I kept thinking, *What does any of this mean? Who is this Lot character who tells a group of men who want to rape his male houseguest that they can rape his daughter instead? Then he gets drunk and sleeps with his daughters? How can this be in the Bible?*

I thought, *It is a holy book, but it's kind of filled with debauchery.* I set it aside. But Sister Anna never set me aside. She lived and breathed love for the Lord. She came to the bars a couple of times with my roommate and me. We talked about the Bible. Well, they did. I had nothing to say really because I'd never read past the first two books. I admired her and was drawn to the inner life of joy she seemed to have even though her existence in the world of the convent and school seemed rather dull to me.

Needless to say, I didn't plan on becoming a nun, but I was strangely drawn to consider Jesus as something more than a historical figure. I remember a pivotal night when emotions of longing and emptiness swept through me and I lay in my bed sobbing. I said something like, *God, there's got to be more to life than what I'm living. I feel empty. I want to know you like Sister Anna does, but how do I do that?*

I'd heard about jobs with the Department of Defense (DoD) where you teach military kids in foreign countries, and I thought if I could go to Europe—they have some huge, beautiful cathedrals—maybe I'd discover God there. I'd read somewhere that cathedrals were built so when one entered, there was a sense of leaving the world and entering another. The height of the ceilings and beauty of the domes overhead made your eyes automatically sweep upward and focus on a higher being. The artwork was to reveal beauty and mystery and story so the soul could open up to the supernatural. I'd read that glorious churches were built for people to better connect with God. Maybe I needed a whole new life away from the familiar to stop making the same bad choices over and over. I asked God if I could get one of those DoD jobs.

He said yes, and off I went to teach school on a naval base . . . in Guantánamo Bay, Cuba. I wondered if He'd heard me wrong. *Cuba? Isn't that a communist country? I don't think they have cathedrals there, Lord. I was thinking Europe, but I'll take what I can get.* For the first time, I was filled with hope that there really was more to life than this, and off I went.

Bachelor Officers Quarters,
Guantanamo Bay Naval Base, Cuba

CHAPTER 2

Changing Worldviews

*I see there is hope,
but can you help me
make better decisions?
Help me to know You.*

I got on an airplane at Chicago O'Hare Airport and flew into Norfolk, Virginia. From there I took a taxi over to the naval base, where I stayed in a hotel. The next day I was to get on a MAC flight (military airplane: C-131) to fly into Guantánamo. I was scared to death. I'd traveled a few times before, but never on my own and never to a destination where there was nobody I knew to meet me and help me. I lay in that hotel room in Norfolk sobbing and chain-smoking. Through the haze of smoke in the air, I looked up at the ceiling and said, *God, if you're really real, I guess it's just you and me now. Help me! I'm scared.*

The next day I sat next to a man named Jerry on the C-131 flight, and we started chatting. Out of the blue, he started telling me God was real and wanted to have a relationship with me through His Son, Jesus Christ. He kind of reminded me of Sister Anna. I realized God had just told me unequivocally, through this man, that

He was real. I also recognized that God Himself had sent this man to help me get settled and not feel so terribly alone. I'd like to say these realizations jolted me into wanting a deeper relationship with God at that point, but old habits die hard. I very quickly made friends with two other young DoD schoolteachers who loved to party. The Officers' Club, a swimming pool, tennis courts, a yacht club (no yachts, just small sailing boats, so not sure why the fancy title), and an outdoor movie theater were within walking distance of the Bachelor Officers' Quarters (BOQ) we lived in. Yes, there were plenty of handsome bachelors who lived there, and plenty more visited the island on ships, arriving for training.

There were very few single women for all these men to date, so life was sweet for us: lots of sunshiny afternoons on the beaches, snorkeling and picnicking, sailing and waterskiing on the bay, happy-hour sing-alongs, dancing on moonlit patios, being wined and dined, and even taking "ship trips" to other Caribbean islands. We were allowed to travel on navy ships going out for training to Haiti, Jamaica, and the Dominican Republic because Guantánamo wasn't open to the rest of Cuba at the time. The "cactus curtain" separated us, so it was like living in a very small fenced-in American town. Because it was considered a hardship tour for DoD schoolteachers, we got some perks, like traveling with the navy or taking embassy flights in order to get away from the seclusion for a bit.

There was a lot of excitement in my life, so why, then, did I have this inner longing for more? In hindsight, I realized that I had prayed for help, and God sent it. Not just in providing an immediate friend in Jerry, but in sending along the handsomest of bachelors when my fooling around was sinking to new lows and I was sick of myself. I met Mike Hawkins at a hail and farewell party. I'd heard about him prior to his arrival on the island. He had quite the reputation of being a hard charger, a Naval Academy grad, but not full of himself like some. I was intrigued when I met him. He was tall and dark, wiry and muscular, handsome in a rugged way. What really interested me, though, was his background. He'd been born in Africa to missionary parents. His family had to leave the Congo when his mom fell desperately ill. They actually got out just prior to major uprisings where many of their compatriots were killed. They ended up in France for many years, so Mike was fluent in French and had traveled all over Europe. His dad joined the air force as a chaplain when Mike was in middle school, so he'd lived in all kinds of places in the States also. He just struck me as so educated and cultured.

We met in December 1981, just prior to my going home to Wisconsin for a long Christmas break. He hung out at the clubs with us, drinking, dancing, singing, and carrying on till all hours, yet he got up every Sunday morning and faithfully went to church. There was only one church building on the base. The Protestants met first, and then the Catholics. Although I was living a crazy life, I still went to Mass every Sunday, and would pass Mike in the parking lot. He'd wave, and sometimes we'd joke about being hungover. But I admired that he was always there. I found out later that he admired that I was singing in the chapel's combined-service Christmas cantata.

We were just friends when I left for Wisconsin for the holidays. He was engaged to someone else back in the States, and I was still somewhat involved with the guitar player I'd been seeing prior to coming to Cuba. But everything changed for me that Christmas.

I'd been getting letters (yes, handwritten letters—no internet or cell phones back then) from some of my brothers and sisters telling me that our brother Tommy had joined a cult. They said he was acting extremely odd, had quit drinking, and couldn't stop talking about Jesus. They begged me to talk some sense into him when I got home. So I wasn't caught off guard when Tommy took me aside and started passionately telling me how he had been saved. My mom thought that Tommy was just going through a phase and would grow out of it. My sisters and brothers thought he was a nut and maybe he'd start drinking again soon and stop annoying everyone. But somehow I knew he was truly changed, filled with an inexplicable joy, and that he would passionately follow his newfound Lord wherever he was called. We talked on and off for the two weeks I was home. I remember telling him after one of the first long nights of intense conversation, "Tommy, I feel like you're dead to me. You're so different. It makes me sad. We used to have so much fun together, and now you're all serious. You've changed so much."

He quoted Scripture back to me. Of course, I didn't know it was Scripture at the time. "You are right Kate. I'm a new creature in Christ. 'It is no longer I who live but Christ who lives in me'" (Galatians 2:20).

What the heck does that mean? Although I was confused, I was finally convinced that Tommy had changed for the better, not the worse. I believed he had found something real and life giving. Something, someone he could give his all to.

Both Tommy and I have intense personalities, and when we do something, we throw ourselves wholeheartedly into it. That's why drinking was such a problem for both of us. We couldn't just have a couple of beers and enjoy the party; we had to drink everything in sight. Tom was a card shark and won lots of money in poker tournaments. He was a top-seeded tennis player, trumpet player, student, and friend. He excelled because if he was going to do it, he was going to be all in. But we both had a restlessness in us, an emptiness that all the pleasures and fun couldn't fill. We talked a lot about that God-shaped vacuum we all have, that Tommy could finally articulate. On the plane back to Cuba, I asked God for help once more. I simply said, *God, show me if Tommy is a nut or if He is right.*

Then came more time spent with the handsome Lieutenant Mike Hawkins. One of my first questions to him when I got back was "What do you think of Jesus freaks?"

Remember this was the eighties, and that's what we called people who were intense about Jesus. I told Mike everything Tommy had said. His response was to ask me if I'd ever read the Bible. I had to admit that I'd only read the first two books. He urged me to read the New Testament and pretty much stated that I would be able to conclude for myself that what Tommy was saying was true. He asked me what I thought being a Christian entailed.

I thought back to a sociology class I'd taken in college where we studied all the major worldviews and religions. I agreed with the ideas of Christianity, but when we started discussing hedonism, I thought, *Hey, that's what I really believe.* My ruling philosophy of life was *Seek pleasure always, and avoid pain no matter the cost. The more fun you have, the better life you will have, and that's it.* Very shallow way of thinking, but as my sister Denny and I used to say, *Don't look for deep waters with us; we are puddles, and we are happy not being introspective or taking life too seriously.* I've since come to understand that you act out of what you really believe, not what you merely say you believe. I constantly sought the party because I was living for pleasure. But once more, I was being challenged to consider a different way of viewing the world.

I read the gospel of John, and then someone sent me the book *More Than a Carpenter,* by Josh McDowell. It was such a logical presentation of who Jesus really was—and is—that by the end of it, I knew without a doubt that Jesus was God and that He came down to earth to save people from their sins. I knew without a doubt that He was alive and wanted to have a real relationship with me. As best as I was able, without any fanfare, I prayed this because Josh McDowell said this prayer helped him and maybe it would help me too:

Lord Jesus, I need you. Thank you for dying on the cross for me. Forgive me and cleanse me. At this very moment I trust you as Savior and Lord. Make me the type of person you created me to be. In Christ's name, amen.[1]

It didn't just help me a bit—it changed me. The prayer had no magic; it was God who changed me. The prayer was just the vehicle I used to open the door of my soul and spirit to the Holy Spirit.

God sent the help I needed to know Him. He sent Jerry and Tommy and Mike and even Josh McDowell. I finally understood what they all were trying to tell me, the thing Sister Anna had tried to communicate to me: that when you surrender to God in faith, He fills you with His love and presence. You don't try to understand it all so you can believe; you believe so you can start understanding it all. In our rebellious, natural state, we scoff at spiritual things and claim that it's all foolishness. It's the Holy Spirit, sent into our spirits when we turn to Him in faith, who gives us the spiritual discernment to understand the things of God.

When I lay in that hotel room in Norfolk smoking cigarettes asking God to help me, I had no idea that He would answer with a gift that wouldn't just help me adjust to a new life in Cuba, but would help me live an abundant life forever here on earth and into eternity. He sent me the gospel of Jesus Christ and opened me up inside to receive and believe that good news. He transformed me from a hedonistic partier into a Spirit-filled Christ-follower. The way I viewed the world was forever changed.

Wiggins Road, Lady's Island, South Carolina

CHAPTER 3

Seeking Healthiness in Body, Soul, and Spirit

*My body feels so sore,
my mind is mushy,
and my emotions are
all over the place.
Would you heal me, Lord?*

Mike and I flew back to Wisconsin and got married in June 1982. We returned to Guantánamo Bay, where we thought we'd stay at least another year, but I got pregnant right away. We needed to either leave prior to my seventh month or stay another full year, as the planes we flew in and out on weren't pressurized, so you couldn't fly with newborn babies. I had prayed that our first duty station together would be a recruiting job in Wisconsin. I was desperately homesick, and when I found out I was pregnant, I just wanted my family around me. I had this new, beautifully intimate relationship with the Lord and was convinced He loved me and therefore should give me what I wanted. When the orders read South Carolina instead of Wisconsin, I was miffed. I started thinking, *Does prayer even work?*

I'd like to tell you that I was young and naïve and grew out of that self-centered, shallow type of thinking, but as my story progresses, you will see I asked that question often, much to my chagrin now. In retrospect, God was answering my prayers—my bigger, spiritual prayers, not my smaller, earthly, comfort prayers.

To help me, He sent me to Cuba instead of Europe. To heal me, He knew it wouldn't happen in Wisconsin. He didn't answer that lower prayer so that He could answer my real need. He wanted to heal my heart from the weight of guilt I was carrying around. He wanted to heal my mind from lies I'd held onto inadvertently. So off I went to South Carolina.

We lived on an island again. This one was called Lady's Island in Beaufort, South Carolina. We brought two baby boys into the world while living there, Michael James and then Matthew Thomas.

Mike's birth was a bit traumatic because I was completely clueless. We took the required Lamaze classes, so I had head knowledge of it all, but actual experience proved that knowledge wasn't enough. I had lots of false labor for a couple of days, which entailed many trips back and forth over the Lady's Island bridge to the naval hospital in Beaufort. We had two cars, an RX-7 sports car and an old beater with no air conditioning. Mike was afraid my water would break on the way to the hospital, so he didn't want to take the good car. Late June in South Carolina is muggy and horribly hot, so by the time they finally admitted me, I was wretchedly worn out.

But I had only just begun what proved to be twenty-four hours of relentless, real labor pains. At one point the midwife claimed she'd have to break my tailbone to get the baby out. We thought we'd have a natural childbirth, which was all the rage at that time, but I started begging for drugs. They wouldn't give me anything all that effective. A little Demerol was all I got after humiliating myself with begging. The breathing thing wasn't really cutting it for me. Mike kept trying to lovingly coach me. He'd say, "Breathe honey . . . breathe." Finally I gripped his hand as hard as I could and yelled, "You breathe! I'm sick of it!"

They finally called another doctor in, who took forceps and yanked Mike out. I remember being completely shocked that a baby could live through all that pushing and pulling and tugging and pain. But he was alive and well. Me? Not so much.

I'd never been so exhausted. I finally got put in a room and was in a deep sound sleep when I heard over the intercom, "All mothers report to the nursery immediately and pick up their babies."

Well, I knew they couldn't possibly mean me, as I was almost dead here. So I rolled over and went back to sleep. Very soon a nurse came pounding on my door admonishing me to go pick up my baby now! I stumbled down the hallway and found Mike in his little plastic see-through bassinet and rolled him back down to my room. I parked him next to the bed and looked down at his sweet little face and begged him to not need anything, as I needed sleep.

I had just fallen asleep again when he started crying. He had his first bowel movement, and it was all tarry and sticky. No one had shown me the equipment on the bottom of the cart that I would need to change diapers—and in my exhausted state, I wasn't thinking clearly. So I wheeled him into the bathroom and took those hard brown paper towels and ran some cold water on them and tried to scrape off the tarry poop. It got all over Mike's little white blanket and all over me. It was a huge mess. I plopped Mike back down into the bassinet and rolled him back to the nursery and whined, "Can somebody help me here?"

The nurses looked disgusted and pointed out the diapers and wipes on the bottom of the cart, but I beseeched them to let me get some sleep. The next morning when the doctor came to visit, I quickly got the impression that the nurses had told him about me.

He had kind of a condescending air about him like he was talking to a simpleton. After all kinds of instructions, he asked if I had any questions. I just had one. Before Mike left me the day before, he reminded me to schedule a circumcision for the baby, so trying to sound mature and responsible and confident, I asked, "When are you going to castrate my baby?"

He said with a smirky smile, "Oh I don't think you want me to do that."

I came right back with, "Oh yes we do! My husband said to be sure and get that castration scheduled."

It was a wonder they actually let me take baby Mike home with me.

Talk about the need for healing! My body hurt, my mind felt spongy, and my emotions were all over the place, from being overwhelmed with love for my new baby to abject fear that I didn't have the ability to care for this fragile new being. My husband's job was really intense, and he was gone all the time, so I felt like it was just me on this island trying to do something really important that I wasn't quite prepared to do. I heard a C. S. Lewis quote once that I loved that definitely applied here: "God whispers to us in our pleasures, speaks to us in our conscience, but shouts to us in our pain: it is His megaphone to rouse a deaf world."[1]

The physical pain I was in passed fairly quickly, as our bodies are so wonderfully constructed by God to naturally heal many of our wounds. But the mental and relational pain I was feeling woke me up to my need for God's touch. I was lonely even with this new lovely little boy in my life. He was joined by Matt the next year, and thankfully, his birth was fairly uneventful. But big Mike continued to work long, hard hours, and family was far away. God seemed to use this time to stir in me the need for a church family. Church to me really meant going to a service and leaving, something you did once a week because it was a sin if you didn't go. I wasn't quite sure why God cared so much about me sitting in a pew each week for an hour. It was this season of my life when I learned that church wasn't me doing a favor for God by showing up. Instead, it was God calling out a gathering of people to be His body here on earth, to huddle once a week to draw strength and celebrate through music, communion, and the preaching of the Word. It was all for the purpose of getting out into the world and making a difference, bringing the gospel of hope to people, helping the poor, encouraging the weak, befriending the confused.

So our little family found a church that met in a school on the island. It was so radically different from what I had experienced growing up, but I loved it. I joined the choir, and we sang all these incredible worship songs that stirred my emotions. The pastor preached sermons I could understand that stirred my mind. I joined a Bible study with two other marine wives and started learning things that blew my mind. All this mental and emotional work led me to set my will to act, to take a step of obedience. I decided to be baptized. The ritual brought some real healing to my soul. The waters of the Beaufort River that I was dunked into held no magical powers themselves, but it was a step of obedience for me to really declare I was all in for the Lord. Up until that point, I was kind of half in, half out.

I was still a huge party girl. We attended lots of social events, and there was always plenty of booze. I didn't go too crazy with it because I was pregnant a lot of the time, but when I could, I indulged. And I was constantly sneaking cigarettes. Mike hated me smoking, and I knew it was bad for me, not to mention my babies, but I was seriously addicted, and quitting during pregnancy each time almost killed me. So as soon as the babies came, I'd start up again, but only in hiding. This of course required lying.

Meanwhile, in this little Bible study, my two friends, who had been Christians forever, were telling me things I'd never heard before. Like the teaching of believers being filled with the Holy Spirit. Our conversation went something like this:

Me: "Are you saying that the Holy Spirit lives inside me?"

Betty: "Yes."

Me: "He is God! Part of the Trinity!" (I knew this because of one part of the Nicene Creed. We used to recite, "I believe in the Holy Spirit, the Lord, the Giver of life, who proceeds from the Father and the Son. With the Father and the Son He is worshiped and glorified." I wondered if Betty knew this.)

Betty: "Yes." (Apparently, she did.)

Me: "Well, if God Himself lives inside me, then why aren't I awesome?"

Betty: (blank look)

Me: "Wait. Do all believers have the Spirit inside them? Do they know it?"

Betty: "It's a major doctrine of Christianity, although there are some different ideas of timing and filling and gifts given, but yes, all born-again Christians have the Holy Spirit inside of them."

Me: "Well then, why aren't our churches awesome? Why aren't they places of love and joy and forgiveness and miracles?"

Betty (paraphrased): "Because we still have free will. We are only as filled with the Spirit of God as we are surrendered to Him. If we are full of ourselves, and many of us are, there's no room inside for Him. We have the power to quench Him, grieve Him, ignore Him, or just stay ignorant of Him. But the whole idea of Christianity is to become like Jesus more and more as you grow spiritually. It's a process. The Holy Spirit in you gives you access to the mind of Christ. He gives you new desires and a purpose for living. He connects you to God and all things spiritual."

This conversation led to another about the ways these women were changing. One of them was getting rid of all her trashy romance novels. I thought that was going a bit far. I liked a bit of trash every now and then. I was worried she would say she was burning them, which made me think of the Nazis and how they burned classics because they didn't agree with the authors. I didn't want to be ugly and narrow minded. Another had decided no R-rated movies. *Really? Why? Aren't they the most exciting?* I didn't want to be a straitlaced, boring kind of person. *Is this what the Holy Spirit does to you?*

I worried that being a Christian would mean lots of rules and being super judgmental and legalistic. Was I seeing my friends go down that path? I knew them, though, and respected them. I gave them the benefit of my doubts and kept studying the Word of God with them. Not just swallowing what they said was true, but scouring Scripture for myself.

I was learning how to study the Bible inductively, which means turning to the Bible first to study what it actually says (observation), then deciphering what it means through word studies and cross references and such (interpretation), and last of all, what it means to me (application). I invested in an expository dictionary, a concordance, Bible commentaries, and a big fat study Bible. I spent hours a day doing my homework, looking at passages of Scripture, and deciphering who, what, when, where, why, and how. Who is writing, and to whom? Why and where are they writing from? What kind of literature is this? What is the main point? I liked this method because it felt like being an investigative reporter for my dad's newspaper. I knew this was a good approach for deciphering the facts of a story. I didn't want to be brainwashed or led astray like people in cults.

A funny thing happened. The more I studied, the more I wanted to study. It was like a hunger and thirst inside me. It was fun and satisfying. I started to lose my taste for trashy romance novels. Sometimes I'd have to turn off the TV, thinking, *This isn't even fun anymore.* And then it hit me that fun could be had in a myriad of ways. I could literally feel my desires changing inside me.

I was quite a good liar prior to coming to Christ. I wanted what I wanted when I wanted it, and if I had to lie to bring it about, well, so be it. But lying got harder. I knew God knew the truth of whatever I'd done, and I felt kind of foolish insisting otherwise. Although I still desired to drink and smoke, I had a stronger desire to be a truth-teller. I wanted to have integrity and be an honest person. I had to keep confessing to Mike that I was smoking or that a friend and I had downed some beers while he was at work. Things were not harmonious in the Hawkins marriage. The pleasure of doing what I thought was fun became kind of a trap. I'd indulged in this kind of behavior for so long that changing felt so hard, like I was losing a part of myself.

This is where the healing began. God showed me clearly that the image I had of myself was not the image He had of me. I thought my identity was wrapped up in being a party girl. *If I stopped all that, would I stop being me?* But God had created me in His image for His glory. He wanted me to find my identity in Him and in the purpose I was created for. One of the only teachings I retained from all the years I went to CCD (Confraternity of Christian Doctrine, kind of like Sunday school for Catholics but on Saturdays) was from the Baltimore Catechism. We had to memorize parts of it. The only part I remembered said, "The chief end of man is to glorify God and learn to enjoy Him forever."[2] I take that to mean the more we get to know God, the more we will enjoy Him (even have fun with Him!), and the more we enjoy Him, the more we will glorify Him.

What does it mean to glorify Him? One way to give someone glory is to give others the correct estimate or opinion of that person. To glorify God means to show other people what He is like by the way you treat them. *How could I ever show people what God is like when I'm this sinful, cynical, wild, loose, selfish, debased party girl? And if this is why I am on earth, I'm in trouble! I can't do this. I want to learn to enjoy Him, but isn't He ashamed of me? I've got so many memories of ugly things I've done.*

The healing came over time. First, He used a conversation with Mike. I'd accused him of being so cocky and prideful, just assuming he'd go to heaven when I could attest to things he was doing wrong! He was startled to find that I didn't really understand the gospel. He explained, "When you receive what Christ did for you on the cross, the price is paid for all your sins—past, present, and future. He removes the debt, covers you, forgives you, and washes you clean. It's as if you've never sinned."

Second, He used a conversation with a woman at Bible study. In response to me confessing how horrible I was and couldn't really be used by God in any significant way, she said, "So, His blood isn't good enough for your sins, Katie? His sacrifice is fine for other people but not you? Your sins are somehow in another category than others'? That's prideful thinking."

Whoa. I thought I was humble. I thought it was Mike who was prideful. But God got through to me that what He'd done for me was to remove the stain of sin, erase it, forget it, and give me a whole new fresh start, beginning with my salvation, but also on a daily basis. His tender mercies are new and fresh every day. And then this gorgeous verse, Colossians 1:27: "It is Christ in you, the hope of glory."

Understanding dawned on me. The Holy Spirit, Christ's Spirit inside me, not only washes me clean of the past but changes my desires in the present and secures my future. He who started a good work in me will be faithful to complete it. He will sanctify my body, soul, and spirit! It's not about me making legalistic choices to appear holy or purchase (earn?) holiness. It's about Him at work inside me, slowly changing me, teaching me, wooing me, and renewing my mind and spirit. The hope I have in being able to glorify God is the fact that Christ is in me doing the hard work of changing me to look more like Him.

My desire to please God started to override my desire to lie and do things harmful to my health and the well-being of my babies, not to mention my marriage. God healed the image I had of myself so I could be a positive, hope-filled person instead of a downcast one. He poured so much love and truth into my fractured soul that true healing came.

Brett Avenue, Fort Knox, Kentucky

CHAPTER 4

Discarding Escapism,
Embracing His Word

Father, I'm spending hours
lost in novels . . . escaping my own
dull life by living vicariously
through other people's stories
and spending very little time
in Your book getting to know
You better. Can You help?

From Lady's Island we moved to Fort Knox, Kentucky. No more islands for a time. I would miss living by the water, but I loved the excitement of moving: getting a new house to make cozy, exploring different territory, and considering new possibilities for adventure and involvement. Unfortunately, the newness wore off quickly, and instead of fulfilling activities, I found loneliness.

I'd beaten loneliness at our last duty station with church friends and Bible study. God had also graced me with friends in other arenas, like a bridge club and the Officers' Wives' Club. He showed me how to replace self-pity with productivity. I had audited a class on computers, which were newly invented, worked on my master's degree in business administration, and participated in tons of social activities our Commanding Officer's wife put together. Life in Kentucky didn't seem to offer any of those opportunities, as we were only going to be there for a six-month school. We went to the base chapel, where I joined the choir, but that didn't take up much time. I met a few of the wives of Mike's buddies who were attending the same school, but all seemed wary of investing much time in friendship since they'd be moving on soon as well.

So I spent all my free time reading novels. It was really like escaping my own dull life for someone else's. I enjoyed it but started feeling like it wasn't really the best use of my time. I recognized it as a kind of self-soothing behavior that wouldn't be helpful in the long run. What would I have to show for it? Most likely just a sense of dissatisfaction with my own life.

I was doing another Precept Bible Study but found myself rushing through that as fast as possible so I could get back to my good novel. One day in the study, we were challenged to give up something that was standing in the way of us getting to know Jesus better. I knew right away that for me it was novels. Now, there is nothing wrong with good novels. They are true gifts from God for us to enjoy. But I'd never even read the Bible all the way through, yet I was plowing through a couple of fiction books a week. I made a commitment that I would not read any secular literature for a year except for *Time* magazine because I didn't want to be ignorant of what was happening in the world. Why I had to be so dramatic and make it such a long time, I don't know. I think it goes back to my all-or-nothing personality type.

For a year I read only the Bible, commentaries, or Christian-themed books. I grew spiritually by leaps and bounds because for the first time I truly was being transformed by the renewing of my mind. Instead of filling my thoughts with the way heroines in my books were being treated, their adventures and romances, their trials and tribulations, I was filling my mind with biblical stories or thought-provoking commentaries on faith. I grew to love biographies of the great saints of old and not-so-old. I ordered a set of Christian classics and read *Practicing the Presence of God* by Brother Lawrence, *The Greatest Thing in the World* by Henry Drummond, and *The Christian's Secret of a Happy Life* by Hannah Whitall Smith—books I never would have chosen because I would have been busy with the latest mystery or *New York Times* bestseller.

Admittedly, after a couple of months, I longed for something lighter to read and became acquainted with Christian historical fiction. A new love affair started. I could improve my mind by learning historical facts, improve my spiritual connection with God by garnering the wisdom presented in these stories, and get emotionally involved in a good plot. But even with these books that fit the parameters of my self-imposed sacrifice, I decided to alternate one serious book with one entertaining book so I would continue to grow spiritually. And each day before I read anything, I started with the Bible in a Year plan. It had readings from the Old Testament, New Testament, Psalms, and Proverbs arranged in a daily dose so that if you were faithful to it, you could read the whole thing in a year. I was determined to be able to say, "Why yes, actually, I have read the whole Bible!" Sister Anna would've been so proud!

I saw God's hand so clearly in this season of my life. I was still a very young Christian. I needed some good, nutritious food for my soul to grow up. He sent me a conviction on how I was spending my free time. Not condemnation that would make me feel bad about myself and hide from Him, but conviction that made me ache to right the wrong and get closer to Him. Then He gave me new desires in my reading habits. I didn't yawn and drudge through serious books anymore. I looked forward to taking in some good wisdom. The self-comforting behavior I was engaging in to make my loneliness recede wasn't what it used to be. I still read a lot! But it was all regenerative to my soul instead of leading me down a path of dissatisfaction with my own lot in life.

God knew I'd need to be able to lean on Him in a deeper way than I was previously able to when I found out I was pregnant for the third time, a couple of weeks before we were due to move again. I started bleeding profusely the night before the movers were coming. The next day I had to go to the emergency room because I knew something was terribly wrong. After a horrible exam by an ER doctor, who I'm quite sure skipped his training in OB-GYN matters, I was admitted, watched for a while, and then sent home with the warning that it might be an ectopic pregnancy, which could be life threatening. By that time all our stuff was packed up, the cleaning team we had hired was at the house, Mike was graduating from the Army Tank School, and we needed to hit the road for our next home in North Carolina. There was no time to heal or weep or even be afraid of impending problems. I took one of our boys in one car, and Mike took the other one in the van, and off we went.

I wanted to feel sorry for myself and pout. I wanted to rage that my husband wasn't properly sad. He kept saying, "Well, thank God. He's sovereign, He knows. You'll be fine." I knew he was just trying to be supportive, but I wanted someone to recognize the drama happening here. I wanted someone to help me deal with this episode. But the few people I knew in the area were also busy moving. Family was far away. If all I'd had at that point to help me with my mixed emotions was the escapism of novels, I'd have been a sorry mess. But because I'd spent so much time with God those past months, I felt His strength pouring into me. I felt His presence. Because He'd convicted me, taught me, opened my eyes further to His immense goodness, I had Him as my real present help in time of need. He showed me I didn't need to rage or pout. I could properly grieve the loss of a little one, and He would comfort me. I didn't need others right then. I had my Hope, my Healer, and my Helper with me always. Boy, would I need Him for what was ahead of me.

Northwoods Drive, Jacksonville, North Carolina

CHAPTER 5

Searching for Truth

Lord, is there such a thing as truth?
How do I know?
My hope is that You will keep me from error,
keep me from weirdness,
keep me from legalism or any ugly behavior
that would hurt Your glorious name.

It wasn't just a miscarriage He was preparing me for, it was ministry. Shortly after settling down in Jacksonville, North Carolina, home to Camp Lejeune, we joined a Baptist church. I finally acquiesced even though I'd previously announced I could never be Baptist in response to Mike stating he could never be Catholic. We had decided not to be affiliated with any one denomination. We would just say we were Christ-followers, and we'd settle into a church that taught the Bible well and had a reputation in the community for being the hands and feet of Jesus. This church in Jacksonville was known for good preaching and a genuine love for the lost and hurting people of our new town. It happened to be a Baptist church. I found a Precept Bible Study to attend at the church, and that was where it all started.

There were maybe a dozen women who gathered weekly and discussed the homework we'd labored over all week. Our leader, Marilyn, was pregnant at the time, and her husband was going to deploy shortly, so she knew she couldn't lead the next semester. To my surprise, she asked me to take over leading. Of all the women attending, I was the least qualified. I still felt like a toddler when it came to spiritual things. She was adamant that I was to be the one. But to lead Precept, you had to have training. The next one was in Goldsboro, North Carolina, and it was a three-day affair, so it involved a hotel room and meals and such on top of the registration fees. When I discussed it with Mike, he said it was out of the question as we were broke, he had no time off to be able to take care of the boys, and he saw no reason for me to do this. Part of me was furious, but then the Spirit in me assured me that if I were to be the leader of this group, I'd get the training I needed. Sure enough, a week later, without me ever nagging about it, Mike brought it up and said we'd make it work if I thought it was important. Off I went to Goldsboro and soaked up so much good teaching.

Within a year, the study exploded with women seeking to understand the Bible. Unknownst to me at the time, an older woman in the area had been praying for ten years that God would send a spiritual revival and stir women's hearts to love Him and His Word. God answered her prayer and used a shaky, insecure person to lead it in the beginning stages—me.

I'll never forget the first time I stood in front of a roomful of maybe eighty women. I had just had another son. I had healed from the miscarriage and got pregnant again very quickly. Jonathan Patrick was two weeks old when we launched the fall season of Bible study. I was scared to death. I looked like a blob with my bloated after-birth body and felt nervous about John being good in his little carrier at my feet. We had childcare for the kids, but he was too little, so I kept him with me. I worried that he'd cry and my milk would flood down in front of everyone. But I'd learned to lean on God; I'd learned that when we are weak, He is strong. I told myself, *You're just a conduit of His Spirit right now, Kate. You can do this because He can do this. You might be a weeping willow right now, but He is a sturdy oak, so just get on with it.*

Well, we got on with it, and the study grew and grew till we had to bring the Precept Ministry trainers to Jacksonville and launch more leaders. My mentor from Parris Island, the fabulous Betty, moved to North Carolina around this time and rented a house in my neighborhood. It was such a provision from the Lord because Mike had to deploy to Japan for six months. So I had support and dear friends all around me. I had three precious sons and a ministry that was thriving. Yet it was a time of confusion. I was so naïve about so many things. Thankfully, the Hope Giver was at work, and I was starting to get a bit of clarity.

The first subject that had me pondering was the role of the Holy Spirit and the gift of speaking in tongues. My brother Tommy spoke in tongues and assured me it was something God had for me too. A pastor I was close to had a very different view. He claimed tongues were from the devil. Now, I've told you some about Tommy. Let me tell you more about him and also about my pastor friend, whom we will call Sam, so that you can clearly see my dilemma of wondering how two godly men could have such completely different views.

Tommy exuded Christ in all he did. He and his wife, Alice, were newlyweds and kind of poor. But when a man in their congregation desperately needed a car so he could get a job, Tommy sold them one of theirs for a dollar. When asked why he would do that when they were barely making ends meet themselves, he said, "Well, I had two cars, and he had none." Who does that except someone totally sold out to Jesus's call to care for the poor? I trusted Tom's heart. I liked the way he was following Jesus.

Sam was a brilliant man. He had three master's degrees, spoke four languages fluently, and had traveled the world as a missionary, church planter, and chaplain in the military. Apparently, he'd had a bad experience with a group of charismatic missionaries in Africa. He said they caused a lot of harm in the villages they were assigned to—how, I don't know; he wouldn't elaborate. Did he surmise from that one experience that speaking in tongues was bad? I think he was too smart for that, but he would never really expound on his position except to say that he believed all the miraculous gifts of the Spirit had ceased with the completion of the canon of Scripture, so anything we were seeing today must be false. What was I supposed to think?

It really was kind of a crisis of faith for me because I wondered if there really was such a thing as truth or if it all just depended on how we interpreted spiritual things. I wanted black and white, right and wrong, truth and lies.

Lord, where is the hope if everything is wishy-washy and left up to what we think? Can't we know?

He answered, *Yes and no.*

What? Isn't that an oxymoron? Through the following months, I felt like He clarified this answer. Yes, there is truth, and we can know it in part while we are here on earth. We can grow surer and surer of His Word and the knowledge of Him. But no, none of us have a complete corner on all truth, and we won't see it all clearly until we get to heaven. In fact, one of the things He hates most is a haughty eye, a prideful heart (Proverbs 6:16–17). I feel like people who insist they are right about every little doctrinal issue and teach every other denomination has it wrong are haughty. I don't want to be like that.

So with humility and earnestness, I asked God to show me the truth about speaking in tongues. I told Him I wanted that gift if He wanted to give it to me. I'd try not to care about my pastor friend thinking I was going over to the dark side. But if that was not a gift for me, I'd try not to worry about Tommy thinking I was missing out. I told God I just wanted to please Him and be totally open to His will in this matter.

That prayer was said early one morning while all my babies were still asleep. That afternoon I got a phone call from a woman in my Bible study. She was an older woman named Bobbie who was a chaplain's wife. That's all I really knew about her. She told me she knew my husband was gone and how hard that can be with three little ones. She said the Lord had laid me on her heart, and she wanted to know if she could bring me dinner. I said absolutely! She brought the most delicious southern cooked meal. I still remember it to this day: fried chicken, green beans cooked in bacon grease, and biscuits and mashed potatoes that were to die for. It was such a gift, since we'd been eating a lot of cereal and macaroni and cheese since Mike left. After we'd eaten and put the kids to bed, she spoke to me.

Bobbie started by telling me she rarely shared her story with anyone unless she knew for sure God was prompting her to do so. That day she became overwhelmed with confidence that she was to tell me everything. I sat wide eyed and all ears as she rolled out the details of what had happened to her and her family. Her husband was a Baptist pastor in a small southern town. He was well loved by his congregation and had an excellent reputation in the community. They lived happily in the rectory with their kids and felt content that this was their life's calling. Bobbie's husband held the same Cessationist views on the gifts of the Spirit as did my friend Sam. Cessationism is a doctrine that purports that spiritual gifts, like tongues, healing, and prophecy, ended shortly after the apostolic age. Her husband preached against the speaking in tongues, and all his listeners said amen.

Then one day Bobbie went to a woman's conference in another town. She said there was a great movement of God among the women, and one of the leaders laid hands on her and was praying over her, when Bobbie opened her mouth and prayed in tongues. Bobbie was shocked, but she knew without a doubt it was a loving gift from her heavenly Father and was beautiful. She went home and told her husband. He said they'd have to divorce if she wouldn't repent of this sin. She begged him to take three days and earnestly seek the Lord about all this. He did, and on day three he also was given the gift of a prayer language in an unknown tongue.

He was excited, and as humbly as he could, he explained from the pulpit the next Sunday that he had been wrong about the gift of tongues. When Bobbie described to me what happened next, I was shocked. Bobbie and her family were run out of town! They were kicked out of the rectory and fired immediately. Within one week they were homeless and jobless. *Wow. The haughtiness, the cruelty of it all.* He eventually joined the navy as a chaplain, and their life calling changed drastically. Instead of a permanent hometown church, they now traveled all over as God and the marine corps led. God told Bobbie to be wise in the telling of her story. Obviously, not all people want to consider that God can impart supernatural gifts to whomever He wants, whenever He wants. However, she felt like I'd be open to hearing.

I quickly shared with Bobbie my recent quandary and my specific plea to God just that morning. She asked if I would like to be prayed over, and I jumped at the chance. I knew without a doubt this was of the Lord. She prayed. I don't remember the words, but I do remember a feeling of liquid heat spreading throughout my whole body. My heart was pounding, and my mind was churning. I opened my mouth and was kind of hoping, kind of fearing that tongues would pour out. Although I made some noises, my mind was saying I was making it up; I was forcing it. My inner voice was also telling me to receive the obvious manifestation of His presence upon me and within me because I certainly couldn't be faking this physical sensation.

Bobbie and I talked about it later. She said God had directly answered my prayer by showering me with His palpable presence and love. That He was pleased with my open attitude and trust in Him, not in what any person would say I had to believe. She felt like I could speak in tongues if I wanted to, but maybe that wouldn't be what would glorify Him best right now. I was satisfied with that answer.

As I went on throughout my life to teach in many Baptist churches, I felt God had given me the task of being a bridge between those who oppose tongues and those who embrace them. I see very clearly both sides, and neither is of the devil. Some of the godliest people I've encountered since my night with Bobbie speak in tongues. I've met some crazy ones too. On the other hand, some of my dearest friends who love the Lord with all their hearts, minds, souls, and strength do not speak in tongues. And then some I've met who speak the loudest against it worry me with their prideful, scornful attitudes.

I want to say to them, do not mock what you don't fully understand. Be grateful for the gifts you were given, and do not belittle the gifts He gave others. Let's be united in one body, intent on one purpose, understanding that it is He who gives the gifts, and the greatest of these is love. You could talk in all the tongues of the world and of the angels, but if you do not have love, you are nothing but a clanging cymbal, making lots of noise and irritating people (1 Corinthians 13:1). Both Tommy and Sam were full of love for others, one gifted with tongues and one not. I could lean doctrinally either way, but what I chose to come away with was a quote I read that made sense: "In essentials, unity; in nonessentials liberty; in all things, charity."[1]

I loved that because in my mind, the answer to my question—Is there hard and fast truth that we can know and stand firm on?—was yes. You find that in the essentials of the faith—the supremacy of God the Father, the gospel of Jesus Christ, and the indwelling of the Holy Spirit. But let's give freedom in the nonessentials. If God is not dogmatic about something in the Bible, how dare we be! One speaks in tongues, one doesn't. One drinks wine, one doesn't. One baptizes infants, one doesn't. And on and on. But in all things, we are given a very clear direction from Jesus to love one another. Love even our enemies. If you think people who speak in tongues are moved by the devil, you'd better love them well then! If you think people who don't speak in tongues are lesser Christians, less holy than you, you'd better love them well then!

Since Tommy and Sam both loved me well, and all three of us had unity in the essentials, the tongues quandary was pretty much put to rest in my soul. We will all know the complete truth of it when we see Him face-to-face, and I'll leave it there. But this loving-well thing became my life's goal.

Unfortunately (or fortunately, depending on your outlook), I came into contact with a couple of people whom I disagreed with wholeheartedly. I wasn't sure how to love them well when I didn't really like them. An older lady in our Bible study had all kinds of opinions and advice for me. She told me that if I allowed my children to trick or treat, I'd be worshiping Satan. I told her my husband had grown up with missionary parents, and he trick or treated and didn't seem to have served the devil. He wanted our kids to trick or treat, so that was good enough for me. She wasn't pleased I hadn't seen things her way. I mentioned the part in the Bible where wives were instructed to honor their husbands, but she said that only counted if they were honoring the Lord, and obviously my husband was not.

She told me that if I made close friends with women in our wives' group who were not following the Lord, I would be sinning because I would become unequally yoked with them, and that was forbidden. I met with these friends on a regular basis, and we had great conversations, lots of weeping, lots of truth and prayer times. Did they convert? Well, not that I know of, but I didn't consider them my project. I simply thought we were to love people and tell them about Jesus. The actual saving part was up to Him. I thought He said go out into the world, not stay in our little Christian bubble of friends. When I tried to reason all this with my Bible study friend, I got some pushback.

But God was trying to stretch me, make me think, not just swallow what anyone said was truth but go to Him and His Word. He kept coming back to the love theme with me. Jesus told us clearly that the most important thing is to love God and love others. In hindsight I realize this woman was probably trying to teach me to follow Jesus the way she had been taught. In her conscience it was wrong to trick or treat and hang out with people who weren't strictly following God. As I recall she got very ill for a time, and I regretted being so quick to judge her. I was filled with an understanding that you never really know what's going on inside people, how they were shaped, what makes them tick. The verse about removing the log from your own eye before trying to remove the speck from someone else's seemed to apply to me (Matthew 7:3). It was easy to judge this woman and feel superior since she seemed so narrow minded. It was another thing to realize she had her own needs and issues, and I hadn't responded entirely with love. I just thought she was wrong and didn't like feeling her disapproval showering over me, so I tried to avoid her. So much for my spiritual depth at the time.

The other person I met whom I strongly disagreed with was a man who was picketing the abortion clinic in town. I'd gotten involved in the local crisis pregnancy center. I had never really cared much about the abortion issue prior to coming to Christ. I'd had several friends who'd had abortions, and I remember thinking, *Well that's good. It's legal, and what else were they supposed to do?*

Then I met a woman in my Bible study who cared passionately about the issue. She had an abortion as a teen, and it left her sterile. She was devastated when she later married and wanted to have kids. Her story was miraculous in that God opened her womb, and she eventually had four children. Her experience led her to have great compassion for women who were pregnant and didn't want to be. It also led her to want to educate young girls and women on what abortion is and does to your body—and soul. So she started a ministry called Birth Choice. It was an amazing place of hope, love, and real help no matter what the clients decided. I loved volunteering there.

But because we were pro-life, we were automatically considered part of the protest movement going on around the abortion clinic in Jacksonville. That clinic was one of only two clinics on the whole East Coast at that time that did late-term abortions. One of my friends was a nurse at the adjacent hospital, and she said the clinic used the lab there at the hospital on weekends. She'd come in on Monday morning and see buckets of dead babies. You could tell they were babies. They were formed enough that no one could call them a random bunch of cells and justify their deaths. But somehow it was rationalized as a good choice. It was a booming business.

Obviously, this was heartbreaking. At first I thought maybe we should protest. I went to the clinic once for a rally, but I was appalled at one leader's behavior. He acted like he hated these women coming for abortions. There was no compassion or kindness. A kind of vileness spewed from him, and he was eventually arrested. I was bewildered and a bit disillusioned. *How can people say they are doing the Lord's work yet have no love in how they talk to people?* I was so utterly naïve in thinking that anyone who said they were a Christian would certainly exhibit the fruit of the Spirit. Not perfectly, of course, but a measure of love and joy and peace and kindness should emanate from them. If they were Christ followers, shouldn't they follow His example? I've always loved the story where the woman caught in adultery was dragged before Jesus (I wonder where, pray tell, was the man? I mean, it takes two!). He said to them as they picked up stones to kill her, "He who has never sinned, go ahead and throw the first stone." They all slunk away. Then he so kindly said to the woman, "No one condemns you? Then neither do I condemn you! Go now and leave your life of sin" (John 8:11).

Jesus didn't hate people who were messing up their lives. He loved them. He just hated when they made harmful, degrading choices. He wanted to help them, heal them, and give them self-respect and connection with His good Father. Shouldn't we do likewise? He was teaching me that I could hate certain behaviors because they harm the people whom God loves but never, ever hate the people. This would be my confession to my Bible study friend and the angry man who picketed: I'm sorry I learned this truth too late and chose only to love the lost friends and the women coming for abortions and not you also. I realize now we are all broken to a certain degree. That's why Christ came, and He isn't finished with any of us yet!

I was also pondering a third thing, which I hinted at earlier in my story, the truth of what prayer is all about in a believer's life. I knew it was important. I knew we were to do it. I knew lots of formal prayers. I knew we could talk with Him conversationally also. It wasn't the asking part that concerned me, but the listening and obtaining answers. I'd read in Scripture that if two or more ask anything in Jesus's name, He would do it. Someone told me that praying "in His name" meant in His will. So in quick succession I asked for things I was sure were His will, and I fully expected an affirmative answer.

A woman in my Bible study confided to me that her husband was having an affair. He wanted a divorce, but she didn't. I responded with great confidence, "Well, we will pray about it, and since divorce isn't God's will and you and I will pray together, then God will make your husband knock it off and love you again."

I was sure of it. The husband moved out and proceeded with the divorce.

Lord? What happened there?

I prayed so hard, along with other volunteers, over certain clients at the pregnancy center. Sometimes it didn't work. Many chose to abort. One woman whom I took into my home temporarily while trying to find a place for her to live ended up stealing from us. She robbed the unwed mother's home where I sent her also. Turned out she wasn't even pregnant, just a scammer.

Lord, we are asking these things in what we believe must be Your will. Why don't You answer? Didn't You promise that You would?

There were other scattered things that didn't play out well. I started thinking something was wrong. *Am I praying wrong? Is He not listening? Did I misinterpret that verse in Scripture?*

Then out of the blue, God miraculously answered something I hadn't even articulated to Him in prayer. One night, I attended a board meeting for the crisis pregnancy center. We had a long debate about going into the community to educate young girls on birth control, STDs, and abortion. I loved the idea of being proactive on this issue instead of just being reactive. It was decided we wouldn't contact the schools and libraries until we had a presentation put together. They all voted to take a year to do this. I was a bit put out that we had to wait a whole year, but I agreed to work on the presentation. Now, keep in mind, this was before computers, the internet, PowerPoint, and so forth. I wrote up a presentation but told the board we needed illustrations. I literally said we need an artist because just stating facts would be boring. It needed to come alive with pictures. The very next day, a woman came into the Birth Choice office and said she'd like to volunteer. I asked what she had in mind, and she said, "Well, I'm an artist."

I showed her the presentation I'd written and asked if she could illustrate it somehow. She got all excited. She said, "I'd love to do this. It would probably take me a year to do it well." I was astounded. The finished works of art were above and beyond all I could have even thought to ask the Lord for. Our presentation was powerful and convincing. Did we help anyone? Not really sure, as I moved shortly after I gave the first one. I mention this because of the question of prayer.

Lord, you don't answer prayers I'm sure are Your will, and then You send a miraculous answer when I didn't really even ask You. I really don't understand the true nature of prayer.

There was never a hard and fast clarity given at the time, just a message to trust Him. Put my hope in Him, not in my own ability to ask correctly. Put my faith in Him alone, not in the outcome of my prayers. If I thought praying was getting Him to do what I said because I knew best, well, that was ridiculous. Praying was getting me to spend time with Him until I understood He knew best. This subject would be revisited over and over throughout my life story. Very soon I was to be tested severely and would continue to fail the test because my current attitude was one of entitlement, not surrender.

Leahy Road, Monterey, California

CHAPTER 6

Acknowledging
the Sovereign
Hand of God

Father, why so many ups and downs in life?
So much beauty, so much pain.
So much kindness, and yet betrayal too.
Fun things turn disastrous.
Gorgeous environments turn dangerous.
Heal my divided soul.
Bring an acceptance and peace
to take the world as it is
and know without a doubt
that You have overcome the world.

California, here we come! Mike had visited his career counselor shortly before deploying to Japan for six months. The guy told him he probably would not be promoted to major, so he needed to carefully consider his next couple of assignments. I was so hurt for Mike, as he was such a dedicated marine, but he took it well and once more assured me that God was sovereign, and we'd be fine.

We decided it would be beneficial for him to get a master's degree to make him more hirable in the civilian world, so he applied to the Naval Postgraduate School in Monterey, California, and was accepted! I was thrilled to be headed to the West Coast for a change.

Two things made that move a tad difficult. The boys all came down with chicken pox, so the glorious cross-country trip we'd planned didn't quite pan out. We spent lots of time swabbing on Calamine lotion and picking up fast food. Not a lot of sightseeing happened, nor the promised glories of swimming in hotel pools every night. I also started feeling queasy and itchy.

I had a strange itching that developed on the backs of my hands each time I was pregnant. John was only nine months old, so certainly I couldn't be pregnant again. I wasn't even done nursing him and back on a monthly cycle yet. Mike was adamant that this would be a terrible time to have another child and maybe we should just quit with the three boys. I had secretly decided I couldn't stop until I had a girl, so I must say I wasn't grieved a bit to find that yes, indeed, I could be pregnant already. Molly Catherine Elizabeth was born in Monterey on February 13, 1989, twenty minutes to midnight. Although I ignored Mike and the doctor urging me to hang on a bit longer so I could have a Valentine's baby, when "Molls" plunged into the world, she became one of my greatest loves of all time.

We'd lived near oceans before, but the Pacific Coast in Monterey was breathtakingly different from the Atlantic and Caribbean shorelines we'd become accustomed to. I think it was the craggy cliffs with little beaches tucked in coves that made it all so gorgeous. Monterey itself made for much adventure with a premier aquarium and Cannery Row (made famous by John Steinbeck in his novel of the same name) and the landscaped walkways up and down the coast road. Our little housing area was up on a hill, and from certain second-story houses, you could see the water. You could hear the sea lions barking every now and then. The weather was ideal in my book: cool mornings when you needed a sweatshirt but hotter in the afternoons when you'd peel it off and then don it once more for the evening chill—never too hot, never too cold. And Mike was home! No deploying or months of being in the field. Life was good!

But with any light-filled paradise on earth, there is always a dark side. Because earth is in a broken state, evil exists. So trials and troubles, big and small, assailed us physically, relationally, and even recreationally. And all things that happen to us have a spiritual impact. As some wise sage said, "We are not human beings having a spiritual experience. We are spiritual beings having a human experience."[1]

I had to keep in mind constantly that Jesus Himself said we'd have trouble in the world, so I shouldn't be surprised or too deeply offended by it. Jesus also said He had overcome the world, and my job was simply to "take heart." (John 16:33) It's not so simple sometimes.

Our physical world was shaken, literally, on October 17, 1989, when a magnitude 6.9 earthquake hit the San Francisco Bay area. I was putting a quiche on the table for dinner. Molly was in her high chair and John in his booster seat. Mike and the older boys were just starting up the stairs from playing outside. It sounded like an airplane was roaring right over our heads. The whole house shook. Molly's high chair bounced across the room as pictures fell off the wall and dishes rattled.

Afterward, the kids thought it was quite an adventure. Everything was canceled for days; electricity was out, so we used candles; and we all slept together on the living room floor and couches. I guess we felt a bit safer being together during all the aftershocks.

That first night, I woke up out of a sound sleep and felt the presence of evil like I'd never felt before or since. I wasn't sure what it was or why it was happening, but I froze with fear. I remembered someone saying that if you sense evil spirits, just start praising God and they will flee. I could barely speak, but I said over and over, "Praise you, Jesus, praise you, Jesus, praise you, Jesus," and whatever was present melted away. I fell back asleep without an ounce of fear. The whole earthquake experience was eye opening. The coast of California is a gorgeous environment but also unstable and somewhat dangerous because of what lies hidden underground.

Like life in general, Lord?

I also had a couple of dicey relationship issues in Monterey. I was in a Bible study with a woman who kept insisting that God gave her specific messages for people. She told me that He had told her to tell another friend that she needed to lose weight and clean up her kitchen. *Really? Does God send messages like that?* When she started telling me what God had told her to tell me, I had to push back. I asked her why God couldn't just come to me directly. Why was she the interpreter? I knew to love her, but I couldn't stand back and have women believing that she had a direct pipeline to God that no one else did and we'd all better listen up to her if we wanted to know what God wanted us to do. I felt like there needed to be some common sense. If what she was saying was opinion based instead of biblically based, then where was the confidence that it was really from God? My relationship with that friend was a bit strained, but we stayed in fellowship with each other, unlike another friend.

A missionary friend dropped me like a hot potato when two things happened. She saw a bottle of wine in our refrigerator and disapproved. That might have been overlooked, but Mike and I turned down the opportunity to support them financially. That was the end. *Hmm, I thought she liked me.* We were prayer partners. Are we to drop people that don't cooperate with our vision of holiness or advance our mission on our time schedule?

Lord, I don't understand what makes certain children of Yours tick. I thought your indwelling presence made us like You. Not perfect, of course, but not dismissive either. I thought missionaries were especially like You. I've got some confusion here.

The help He sent was by way of a simple analogy. I read somewhere that often spiritual truths mirror physical truths. Physically people are born as babies, obviously, and as they grow, they change and hopefully mature. Babies can't do much but poop and pee and cry and eat. They need a lot of help to thrive and survive. Toddlers fall down a lot as they are learning to walk. Elementary kids get a lot of things wrong, and teenagers can be totally obnoxious in thinking they are right about everything. But these stages pass, and hopefully, maturity comes. So spiritually, when a person is newly born again, it isn't wrong of them to need a lot of help in starting to grow. When a person is a spiritual toddler, they're going to fall down a lot. During the elementary years of being a Christ follower, they are going to get a lot of things wrong. And sometimes Christians who think they know everything and couldn't possibly be wrong might just be going through a teenage phase in their walk. Bottom line, God was showing me that all Christians are at different places in their walks, learning different lessons at different times, maturing in various lessons at different rates, and that my responsibility is to continually love others as He has loved me.

Jesus didn't come to condemn the world but to save the world. He is our example in how we treat others. I didn't need to condemn the woman spouting what I thought was nonsense or the woman whom I felt had weighed me and found me wanting. I needed a deep understanding that just because people are trying to follow Christ doesn't put them in a category of perfection. When they are unkind or pompous, it's not that they are hypocrites, as the world loves to say; it's that they are works in progress, slowly growing up into the likeness of Jesus. You'd think we'd all know this because we know ourselves!

God showed me I could be offended by my friends or I could be gracious to them and learn from them. From the one who acted as a confident modern-day prophet, I learned if I could not back something up from Scripture that I wanted to communicate to someone, I would simply state it as my opinion. Then I would leave it up to that person as to whether they felt like it was an opinion worth taking seriously. If God was behind the message in any way, I'd leave it up to Him to convince His own child. And from the missionary friend who ditched me, I learned to not take it personally if someone wasn't supportive of whatever ministry I was involved in. I learned not to judge others on appearances. That bottle of wine in my refrigerator was actually sparkling cider. If she had asked me about it and honestly said it bothered her, I would've explained. Instead she told a mutual friend it was one of the reasons she needed to part ways with me.

This next area of trials is going to seem ridiculous to some, but I think it's worth mentioning. We had trials and tribulations related to recreation. Every time I planned something fun to start building memories with our kids, something dire would befall us, and the fun turned "unfun."

I loved camping as a girl. My fondest memories were gathering with relatives at campgrounds and spending long summer days swimming, playing games, and running free and cooler nights around a campfire singing and storytelling. So we invested in camping gear and sought the nearest campground. The Laguna Seca Raceway and Campground sounded exotic—it was near the ocean, after all. But reality didn't match the fantasy. It was on a sandy dune, so no trees, no shade, and no soft grass to put the tent on. Also, the ocean wasn't really in sight. You had to cross a busy freeway to get to it. Molly was a baby, and John didn't walk well yet; he mostly crawled. So we either had to hold him or let him crawl in dirty, rocky sand. There was no pool, camp store, rec center, and certainly no relatives. There weren't even other campers to interact with. Apparently, it was just a place to camp if you wanted to watch the races, but there weren't any of those going on. It was a very dull experience.

We tried again another weekend thinking we had just picked the wrong campground and needed more people along. So off we went to Big Sur with some friends and their kids. The hike we took after setting up camp was fabulous, but it started raining. We were determined it would pass, but it only came down harder and harder until our tent was a river, and we had to pack up and go home.

Maybe just staying in hotels would be better until the kids were older, so I booked a weekend near Hearst Castle. I packed a picnic, and we were going to drive down the Pacific Coast Highway from Monterey to San Simeon. The views of the ocean along this patch of road are off the charts, at least when it's not foggy. The day we left was so closed in with fog, you literally could not see in front of you. The highway twists and turns upon high cliffs with narrow shoulders and huge drop-offs to the crashing waves below. Mike has a lead foot and views driving as a competitive sport. Within an hour we were all carsick and scared. We couldn't stop along the way for the picnic as planned because of the soggy weather. Mike commanded that we eat the sandwiches in the car. *Who in their right mind can eat egg salad and Fritos while lunging around curves and visualizing going over the side? Well,* I thought, *certainly once the nightmare trip ends at the Hearst Castle for a tour, the fun will start.*

Oh my!

First the fog turned into a downpour. Who said it never rains in California? Molly was tucked into a backpack to try to keep her dry, but the rest of us got soaked as we toured the grounds. Once inside the castle, all hell broke loose. Mike had recently gotten contacts, and one of them rolled up into the top of his eyeball, and he could not get it out. His head was pounding. The castle had a runner you were supposed to stay on as you toured. If you stepped off the runner, an alarm would sound, and you'd be warned to stay on the path by your guide. Well, imagine little boys who have just been cooped up in a car obeying the runner law. No. It became a game for them. They loved making the floor buzz. Mike was in agony trying to corral them.

Well, there was still the luxury of a hotel and a nice meal ahead of us. The hotel turned out to be only functional, and the meal was McDonald's eaten on the hard beds in the lackluster room.

Oh Lord, what kind of memories am I building for my kids?

Thank goodness there was no Facebook or Instagram back then. Our photos would have been of kids crying, me drenched, unappealing meals, and Mike taking Tylenol.

The last trial we encountered in paradise was as we were leaving it. Weeks before the movers arrived, we were issued orders to our dream job and location in Annapolis, Maryland. Mike was a Naval Academy grad, and we had visited there on our honeymoon. I fell in love with the little downtown area, the grounds of the academy, the architecture and history of the place, and the setting right on the waters of the Severn River and Chesapeake Bay. Mike was assigned to be a math instructor, which was great, but the real joy in his eyes was the opportunity to be an assistant coach for the rugby team. He had played rugby all four years at the academy, and he was so excited to have the game be part of his life again. I was excited for him. If he was going to have to get out of the military at the end of this tour, then let this next season be fabulous for him and for me too.

I envisioned a cozy little house near the bay with a glorious view within walking distance of the little shops and restaurants in the town. I saw myself and the four kids swimming and sailing and window shopping and attending parades and rugby matches. If Monterey was paradise with a dark side, Annapolis was going to be heaven with no shades of hell anywhere!

And then we were betrayed. Mike hates it when I word it like that, but it sure felt like a betrayal to me. There were three men, including Mike, getting a master's degree in applied mathematics from the Naval Postgraduate School. There were three jobs to be filled after their graduation. Mike was assigned the one in Annapolis until one of the other guys decided he wanted that job instead of the one he was assigned to. He made some phone calls. He called in favors from the higher-ups. At the last minute, our orders were canceled and reissued to us to head to Washington, DC, where Mike would work at Headquarters Marine Corps. And our supposed friend was now going to the wonderful academy at Annapolis. Oh, I was mad! I was crushed. I was hurt. Why would our friend go behind our backs and steal our job? But it was more than that. I was offended with God. I felt like He'd held out a good gift to me and then yanked it away at the last minute. I know now how selfish and small that attitude was, but at the time, it was genuinely how I felt. I had prayed and prayed that we'd get the academy job. We got it, and I praised Him effusively. But then we didn't get it.

Lord Jesus, what is happening? Are You not a good gift giver? Are you possibly toying with me?

Mike's standard answer was "Kate, God is sovereign. He knows what He's doing. We will be fine."

Ugh! Why does he always have to say that? Well, maybe because he speaks the truth in love to his immature wife! I can't wait to tell you the end of this story, but like most stories, a lot had to happen before the resolution was clear. Like all stories, at least the good ones, there was conflict and trials and death and evil, but also hope and love and, in the end, rescue. Washington, DC, awaited us.

Setter Place, Springfield, Virginia

CHAPTER 7

Rejoicing in Terrible, Wonderful Things

*Jesus, I think I might have married
the wrong person, but I don't think
divorce is an option. Can you give me some
hope in this troubled marriage?
My dad is dying of cancer;
please God, heal him now, as I can't bear it!
I'm in over my head in ministry. Help!*

I eventually realized that God hadn't let us down by sending us to DC. He had bigger plans for us than coaching rugby and swimming and sailing on the Chesapeake Bay. As wonderful as all that sounded in our imaginations, we had a different kind of wonderful presented to us: marriage problems, the death of my beloved father, and a ministry that was completely out of my comfort zone. How could any of those scary, hard things be any kind of wonderful? God used them greatly to grow us.

A lot happened in DC that probably wouldn't have in Annapolis. The guy who stole our job ended up divorced and was passed over for promotion. Mike and I had lots of time to work on our marriage, and Mike's job at headquarters helped him earn a promotion. I'm not delighting in the guy's downfall, although I do think cheaters never prosper. I'm kidding. He didn't really cheat; he just grabbed what he wanted for himself because he had the connections to do so.

I mention this because we also had connections. Our connection with God didn't give us what we wanted but what we needed. We might have divorced also if we'd had three crucial years of Mike being on the road all the time with a rugby team known for partying. We needed time together and friends and a good church home. Mike didn't need a tour of duty that took him away from decision makers that sit on promotion boards but a job that kept him in the limelight. My desire for life in Annapolis wasn't wrong, just shortsighted, kind of like when I ached to go to Wisconsin for our first tour together. Our Father in heaven knew better both times. Boy, I wish now that my young self could have embraced that fully and trusted Him wholly. All in good time, I guess.

Let's start with the new neighborhood. We found a beautiful house on a cul-de-sac in the Orange Hunt area of Springfield, Virginia, about a half-hour drive from the Pentagon and Marine Corps Headquarters in DC. As we turned onto Setter Place, there were a whole bunch of kids on bikes that waved and followed us down the street to our new house. As our kids tumbled out of the van, the neighborhood kids introduced themselves and welcomed us. Apparently, the couple we were renting from had alerted all the neighbors as to the time of our arrival. Shortly thereafter, home-made macaroni and cheese, apple pie, a bottle of wine, and the parents of the kids showed up. What a great start to a new place.

We'd heard of a dynamic church from Mike's brother, Jim, who had previously been stationed in DC, so after unpacking boxes and settling in, we headed to Immanuel Bible Church. I met a couple of women in a class for newbies, and we started our own little encouragement group. We bonded quickly, and that group of women became a great source of joy for me. We all joined a Sunday school class together so our husbands could meet, and we quickly made more friends. That group did so many fun things together, like river rafting, dinner parties, picnics, concerts, and such. I was invited to lead a Bible study group and be on the women's ministry board. I met more incredible women through those two venues. I started taking counseling courses through the church along with leadership development classes. Mike and I led an AWANA group for kids that was a lot of fun. These were the easy, wonderful things.

But when things are nothing but easy, you don't need the Lord much. You may pray and read your Bible and go to church and such, but it's the harder times that really cause you to lean into Him. So He allows trials and tribulations. I honestly don't think He sends them. We cause a lot of them ourselves by our sinful, broken ways of dealing with each other. Also, there's the reality of life on earth, which includes sickness and death, that brings sorrow.

Let's talk about the sinfulness. Mike and I were fighting like crazy. I was horrified about it and honestly had decided I'd married the wrong person. I wasn't sure what to do about it though. My own parents never fought in front of us when we were kids. I remember one time that they weren't speaking to each other over something, and I went to my room after a silent dinner and cried. My mom came in and asked what was wrong with me. I looked at her in disbelief that she could even wonder and said, "You are going to get a divorce now, and I have to decide who I'm going to choose to live with."

She got mad at me for being so dramatic. She said they were just having a difference of opinion about something, and I didn't need to make it more than it was. I was offended and said, "Fine! I choose Dad!"

Yes, I was dramatic then because I was a kid, but as an adult I didn't think I was overstating my incompatibility with Mike. We disagreed on so many things. The two biggies were how we'd spend our time and our money. He was frugal in little things. I was not. I loved going out to eat, buying the kids treats, getting my hair done, and things like that. I could nickel-and-dime us to death. He gave me a strict budget that I thought was ridiculous. I felt powerless to change it, so resentment built up in me week by week. Then he eagerly spent money on big things, like new cars every couple of years. That made me nervous. My dad would buy a used station wagon, and we'd drive it till it was dead. Then he'd get another used one. *Why couldn't my husband be like my dad? Then we'd have more money to do the things I thought were best!*

I was a more-the-merrier type of hostess; he was a one-couple-at-a-time kind of guy. I loved going to other people's parties. He only went when he had to for some reason.

I was crazy about my extended family and wanted to see them often. He insisted we had our own family now, and that was all we needed. He never expected to see much of his own extended family, as they were all military and lived around the world. So it just wasn't a priority in his eyes to spend time with brothers, sisters, and parents.

He was extremely neat and tidy and organized. I was sloppy and disorganized. He was a planner. I was spontaneous. I liked to dance. He hated it. He liked gardening. I couldn't have cared less about yard work. He freely expressed irritation and anger. I suppressed it and became passive-aggressive. And on it went.

I realize it might not sound like much as I try to explain this, but I wasn't happy in my marriage. I couldn't divorce him; we'd promised each other that we'd never even consider that as an option. Plus, we had four precious kids, and although we didn't get along, he was a great dad. I could never be so selfish that I'd take the kids' dad away from them. I went to a counselor and pretended that I was asking his advice for a friend. Of course, he saw right through my ruse. When I explained everything happening, he said, "Your 'friends' will probably hang in there for another decade or so till the kids are older, but in the end they will divorce. It sounds inevitable."

Well, that was encouraging!

As I recount this, I see the selfish sinfulness in both of us. We wanted things done our way, in our time, at all times. We couldn't understand why the other couldn't just agree. I'd read Philippians 2:3, which said, "Do nothing from selfishness or empty conceit, but with humility consider one another as more important than yourself." It goes on to say we are to have the same attitude in ourselves that was in Christ Jesus, that although He was God, He didn't hang on to the rights due deity, but humbled Himself and became a servant, even unto death. So I decided I had to always consider Mike as more important than me and just be a servant unto death. The problem was I truly wanted to hang on to my perceived rights! Plus, I kept wondering, if Mike was a Christian, why couldn't he consider me as more important than him? I knew that two shall become one in marriage, but why did he get to be the one we became? The only conclusion I could come to was that he wasn't studying Scripture as hard as I was, so I had to be the bigger person and act more like Jesus. But gritting my teeth and deciding I had to bear up until death was not a healthy way to be married. It was a poor application of Scripture on my part, but I didn't know that at the time. Jesus wasn't obedient to other people, only to His Father, which sometimes meant He stood up to other people and opposed them or walked away if they were toxic.

During all this marriage dysfunction, our country went to war with Iraq. Mike begged his assignments monitor to send him to the front lines. He was eager to get in the fight. My friends were appalled.

They felt bad for me. Truth be told, at that point I was eager for him to go. He wanted to go do what he'd been training to do for years, and I wanted to have some freedom to spend money and visit family and socialize with none of the tension attached. When his orders to Iraq came through, we were both happy. But the war ended before he got over there. It was at this point when I begged God for help.

He sent it in various ways. One was through a marriage conference. I wasn't excited about it at first because I had dragged Mike to one in Monterey, and it had been a disaster. But our friends from the Sunday school group were all going, and the peer pressure helped get us there. In my sinful pride I wanted Mike to be convicted of all the wrong he was doing. But in God's delightful way, I was the one who was deeply convicted. He used a personality test, the Myers-Briggs assessment,[1] to show me that Mike was wired completely opposite in every way from the way I was wired.

The whole conference was based on "different is not wrong." It's just different. Loving one another when you are different is not easy, but we have the Holy Spirit in us and the fruit of relying on Him is—first and foremost—love. I learned that love is a decision, not a feeling. It's a choice to be filled with the Spirit so we can love God, love ourselves appropriately, and then love others unconditionally. Oh my, there was so much to learn! That basic teaching was radical to me. It really changed my whole perspective on Mike's way of doing life. I realized he was not wrong. He was not insane. He was just different, and that was okay. It was prideful to think my way was always the right way. God is opposed to the proud but gives grace to the humble (James 4:6). I was completely humbled at that weekend conference. The cool thing is that Mike was too! We both apologized to each other for the selfish ways in which we'd been behaving and the negative thoughts we'd been harboring toward each other. It was so cathartic and life changing.

God also used my journaling and Bible reading habits to communicate to me His views of how to love others well. I clearly recall a morning as I sat pouring my heart out to God about Mike in my journal. Flipping back to earlier entries, I realized I was doing a lot of complaining about him. But I felt justified because I thought, *If I write down all the wrong things he's doing, then the next time we have a fight, I will remember them all and be able to bring them up and point out how he needs to change.* Then I picked up the Bible I was using for daily devotions and happened to be in the New Testament book of 1 Corinthians, chapter 13, to be exact. If you are familiar with this famous section of Scripture, it is very convicting. It starts out by saying something like: you can be the most talented, gifted, generous, religious person in the world, but if you don't have love, you are absolutely nothing. And then it goes on to explain very succinctly that love is not an emotion but is acted out. "Love is patient, love is kind, love does not keep a record of wrongs" . . . That leaped off the page to me.

I had the audacity to argue with God. I said something like *Well God, I know it says I shouldn't be writing down every wrong thing Mike does, but I think it's a good idea. Don't You see that this could help our marriage get better? He needs to change, and I need a tool to help him see that!*

Oh my goodness, over and over the powerful Word of God resonated in me. Love is patient and kind. It doesn't bear a grudge, and it doesn't keep a record of wrongs. It's never rude or boastful. It bears all things, believes all things, hopes all things, endures all things. And without it, you are nothing! I knew God, in His infinite love for me, was urging me to trust His wisdom here and not rely on my own understanding of what I thought would improve things.

I could certainly choose to act patient even when I didn't feel patient. I could choose to react kindly to situations instead of with a haughty spirit. I could quit journaling every little offense and start dwelling on all the good and hopeful qualities in my husband. I could give him the same kind of grace that God was lavishing on me despite all my wrongdoing. I asked God for the strength and wisdom and inner power to love Mike well. And slowly but surely, God provided!

You know that verse that says you reap what you sow? Over the years I sowed patience and kindness and hopefulness, and I have reaped such beautiful love from Mike in return. Turns out I didn't marry the wrong guy after all! And I was the right woman for Mike, too, despite our being polar opposites. We just both needed God to help us adjust our attitudes and perspectives in the way we viewed one another and His power to make different choices in how we would choose to treat one another going forward.

On to the next terrible, wonderful thing—my beloved dad had cancer. It was bad—in his liver, lungs, and brain. My prayer at the time was *Please God, heal Dad. I don't want to be on earth without my dad. I'm not sure at this point if Dad will be in heaven either. Heal, help, and give me hope, God!*

Dad had boldly stated that he didn't need a Savior because he could save himself, thank you anyway. And if any human being could save himself, it would have been my dad. He was a great guy, a loving, faithful husband, an attentive dad, a hardworking provider, a source of intelligence and righteousness in the community, and a genuinely fun-loving, kind, generous person to hang out with. He was dearly loved by many, went to church regularly, tithed, and said his prayers.

So why did I think he might not go to heaven? Because the Bible makes it very clear that all have sinned and fallen short of the glory of God (Romans 3:23) and that the wages of sin is death and eternal separation from a holy God (Romans 6:23). It's made clear that we are saved by grace through faith, which is a gift from God, not a result of works, lest any man should boast (Ephesians 2:8–9). Dad was convinced he could earn his way to heaven with his good works and religious acts. But I was convinced that he needed Jesus, not just an intellectual relationship with the belief that Jesus indeed existed as the Son of God and died on the cross for us—Dad believed that—but a heartfelt, surrendered relationship to Jesus and a true belief of why He came. He came because we all need a Savior, even morally upright people like Dad.

I heard an analogy one time that made sense to me. It's like we are all in the ocean of life desperately trying to swim to shore. It's tiring. It's hard. God comes along and throws us a life preserver (Jesus) and says, "Hang on tight to Him, and I'll pull you in."

The thing is, many of us turn away and say, "No thanks. I'm a pretty good swimmer. I'll make it on my own."

And we can for quite a while. But the sharks come, and the thirst gets excruciating, and no matter how strong we are, it's never enough. God urges us to grab hold and be saved. But He doesn't insist. He has given us all free will.

Anyway, I found myself in a wrestling match with God. I wanted Dad to be healed because I wanted to enjoy him for many more years on earth. I wanted him to be Grandpa to my kids. I loved him so much that I thought, *If God loves me, He will realize He needs to heal my dad.* For six months I prayed in this vein to no avail. Dad was dying. I got the call to come home immediately if I wanted to say goodbye to him. I remember vividly my conversation with God on the airplane.

What are You doing? Why wouldn't you heal my dad? You healed Mom (a story I haven't shared yet!), so why not Dad? And will Dad go to heaven? I can't live if he dies and goes to hell because he couldn't lay down his pride and receive what You did for him on the cross. I'll never laugh again. I'll never have joy. How could I? How heartless would I be to enjoy life while envisioning Dad suffering for eternity? God! Please!

I didn't hear an audible voice in response, but a still small voice inside me said, *Trust Me.*

That's it. No explanation. No apology. No promises. Just *Trust Me.* And the funny thing is, I did. Right at the moment of my tears and frustration and anger and fear, He met me with calming words, *Trust Me.* Nothing had really changed in the situation I was facing, but everything within my soul changed. He'd given me peace, not as the world gives by fixing everything to my liking, but as He gives, an inner reassurance that I don't have to have everything figured out. He's got it. There's my hope.

Dad lived for two more weeks, and it was one of the most meaningful times in my whole life. All my siblings came home. We rented a hospital bed and set it up in the living room so the foot of it was facing the piano. My sister, Denise, would sit on the edge of the bed and play Dad's favorite songs, and we'd sing along. I don't have a great voice and always sang alto or tenor, but as we sang to Dad, these lovely high notes were coming out of me. That sounds odd, but I looked up and asked God if He'd sent an angel to comfort us. It was a capricious thought and comment, but something supernatural seemed to be happening.

That idea got confirmation when Denise and I went off to the store to buy adult diapers, as we could no longer lift Dad up to get him to the bathroom. She told me that she hadn't played the piano much these past years and wasn't that good when she used to play, but now her fingers were just flying over the keys, and she wasn't missing notes. She said it felt like she was playing on a higher plane, or something inexplicable. I told her about the soprano voice floating out of me. We were both in awe. Later our brother, Jimmy, told us that when he was playing his trombone at Dad's funeral (we had a family Dixieland band play at the reception afterward), he was hitting notes he'd never been able to before. He said it felt like something was empowering him. The message from God was clear to me.

I'm with you! I'm for you. I feel your pain, and I want you to know my comfort. Music is a good gift from me and can soothe souls.

But the best thing happened one night when I was on nursing duty. We all took turns in shifts of two, sleeping on the couches near Dad, so if he ever needed anything, we'd be right there. I was dozing on and off, and I heard him cry out, "Okay, what's the barrier to God?"

I jumped off the couch and sat next to him. I said something like "Dad, there's no barrier except for the ones we erect. You just need to trust in what Jesus did on the cross instead of in your own goodness or religion."

He said, "Okay, I want to do that. What do I need to do?"

I said, "Well, you just pray and tell God what you're thinking and feeling and tell Him you surrender your pride in your own ways and embrace His way of the cross. Ask Him to save you, and He will."

Dad said, "I don't really know how to do that."

So I said, "How about if I pray the words, and you pray along in your heart if it sounds like what you want to express to God?"

We prayed together, and Dad joyously said, "Amen!"

And then he said, "I have to tell Janet I changed my mind."

And I knew he was talking about how adamant he and Mom had been against Tommy's and my assertion that people needed to receive Jesus for who He is and believe that what He did on the cross was to pay the price for their sins. They both thought Tommy and I had defected to the other side (Catholic vs. Protestant). When I told my parents that Mike and I were not going to be

Catholic, per se, just Christ followers who embrace ecumenicalism, my dad cried. He told me my forefathers had fought and died for the faith, and now I was just throwing it away and embracing the "enemy," if you will. I argued back that it shouldn't be about loyalty to a denomination but faithfulness to God and Jesus, and I was wholeheartedly going to be about that.

I wish I'd been more well read at the time and could have said it wasn't really religious teachings that separated the Protestants and the Catholics in Ireland. They believe in the same God. It was primarily a social and cultural conflict. But I digress. The point is, Dad had found peace, and he wanted to tell my mom that they were wrong in judging Tom and me as being foolish and somehow against their religion. (Although when Tommy was brand new to his faith, he did tell them he thought the pope was the antichrist, so that didn't sit well! It was very understandable that there was the perception of us against them. Tom later apologized and said he was young, excited, and naïve—and a bit mouthy back then.)

After praying with Dad, I worried that I hadn't made the gospel clear, that somehow I'd messed up this important moment. I didn't really mention sin. How can it be the gospel if you don't recognize you're a sinner in need of a Savior? How shallow I was in thinking I had to get it right for there to be a movement of the Holy Spirit in someone else? But truth be told, I was shallow! God, in His infinite tenderness, sent beautiful confirmation to me in three different ways.

For one, Tom told me that the next morning during his devotional when he started praying for Dad, like he'd been doing every day for the last year, begging God for healing of body and/ or new life in Christ, God whispered to him, *It's done. You can stop asking.* Tom felt a heaviness lift off him and a joy but didn't really know what to expect. I remember dragging him into the laundry room and explaining my conversation and prayer with Dad, and he got so excited. He assured me God doesn't need our paltry presentation of the gospel to get His truth across to someone. It's a supernatural work, not a natural one. It wasn't me trying to sell Dad something. Although my mom later accused me of putting words in a dying man's mouth. She said Tom and I were little snots who thought we knew it all, and Dad was holier in his lifetime than we ever had any chance of being. Let's just say Mom didn't take it well when she was told that Dad wanted her to know he'd changed his mind!

The second thing God did was speak to me through His Word during Mass that next day. The first reading was from 2 Corinthians 4:16 (NASB): "Therefore we do not lose heart, but though our outer man is decaying, yet our inner man is being renewed day by day." I felt like that was a direct word from God to me. Dad's body was giving out, but his soul was revived.

The third confirmation I had was Dad's behavior. It wasn't just my imagination or my hopeful thinking. The next day he was so changed in his spirit. Prior to praying together, he was very restless and kept repeating that he was going to beat this thing, even though the doctors had said there was no hope for healing. He had seemed agitated and kind of angry and determined that he would make himself better. My dad was used to bringing about results through hard work and determination. But cancer is such an evil thing, and death can't be beat by our human strivings. It's the great leveler. I believe Dad knew this in his soul, and it scared him. That fear evaporated when he trusted Christ. He loved to sing and make music, and Dixieland had always been a favorite genre of his, but now he wanted to hear songs like "Amazing Grace." He also wanted us to sing over and over a song we used to sing during the Mass that is based on John 11:25: "I am the resurrection and the life, he who believes in me will never die."

Another favorite Dad wanted to hear was "Just a Closer Walk with Thee." I didn't know it was the most frequently played number in the hymn and dirge section of traditional New Orleans jazz funerals. We had it played at Dad's funeral. The song talks about when our feeble lives are over, we will just be in a more intimate, face-to-face walk with Him.[2]

———— ⁍⧫ ⧫⧨ ————

So beautiful, so comforting. Not only the songs and the spiritual movement happening, but the relational healing that happened between Dad and me was a gift. Once we had made the decision to get diapers for him, someone obviously had to change him, and that someone was me. We had a little family meeting, and nobody else felt like they were up to the task. I am normally kind of a wimp and wasn't sure I could do it either, but I kept feeling God's presence and power in a new way, so I volunteered. It was so incredible. I thought it would be yucky, but it gave us a tender time to talk. At first Dad was embarrassed and kept saying he was so sorry to be such a nuisance. I sincerely said to him, "Dad you changed my diapers at the beginning of my life. I am so honored to get to repay you for all that good care you gave me, so now it's just my turn to change you. It's a privilege, Dad, so please don't think twice about it!" He accepted that, and for the week or more of doing my job, we chatted in such a heartfelt, real way.

I had given Dad a lot of grief in my teen years. At one point he was so frustrated with me that he beat me. He was never a violent man at all, but I had pushed him to the limit. One night I came in four hours after curfew, and I had a flippant attitude about it. He couldn't take it anymore and lost his temper big-time. It bothered him for years that he hadn't had more self-control that night. And it bothered me that I had driven him to distraction. He and I had such a good, honest, cleansing conversation about all that. And when he told me how much he loved me, I cried and cried because he said it so tenderly. I could tell he was desperate for me to understand and accept how deeply he meant it.

See what I mean about both terrible and wonderful? How terrible to have to change your father's diapers (and for him to be changed by his daughter!), and yet how wonderful to be in a place where heartfelt conversation could take place. We truly can hold joy and sorrow at the same time. Jesus did. He said for the joy set before Him, He endured the cross (Hebrews 12:2). He promised through the apostle Paul that He would work all things together for good for those who love Him and are called according to His purposes (Romans 8:28).

Dad's funeral was packed, and the reception afterward was a huge party. We truly celebrated a great life with my brothers and sisters playing Dixieland music and all the grandkids dancing, laughing, and running around. For two more nights my siblings and I stayed together with Mom and talked and talked into the wee hours of the morning. There were lots of tears but lots of funny stories and laughter too. My brother, Jimmy, said he saw my and Tom's faith in a new light. He realized we had a comfort that was beyond this world. His respect felt like another healing gift given in my sadness.

When I got back to Springfield, I didn't know how the grieving process would go with me. I'd never experienced real grief before. I did two things that helped. Well, one thing I did, and one thing I believe God did.

I had a dear friend, Cathy, who lived across the street. She and I decided to fast together one day a week and pray for the healing of broken hearts: my own, my siblings', but especially my mother's. Mom confessed to me that she had considered taking an overdose of the pills that were prescribed to my father and just ending her life. She was so bereft without her soul mate. It tore me apart to think of my mom in so much pain. I begged her to come stay with me, but she wasn't comfortable at my house. I regretted that, but it was just the reality. She was a chain smoker, and she knew that Mike wasn't wild about smoke in the house. We didn't keep beer or booze in the house either, and she liked a drink or two. She went and stayed with each of my sisters, Sheila and Denise, which relieved me. I have to admit I was a little jealous; I wanted her to love me too. But it wasn't about what I wanted at that time.

Since I couldn't comfort her in person, all I could really do was intercede for her in a way I felt was more powerful than just praying. So my neighbor, Cathy, and I fasted every Sunday. When I'd get a pang of hunger, I'd beseech God to heal Mom. Having someone fasting with me helped me stay committed. Mom eventually started to live and laugh again. Did the praying and fasting help hasten the day? I can't be sure, but I do know that Scripture says the prayers of the righteous availeth much (James 5:16). We are urged to pray for one another, bear one another's burdens, and weep with one another. Fasting was simply a way I could stay focused and remember to take my emotional pain (and the pain of others) to the One who heals.

The thing that God did for me, which might sound odd, was to send me dreams of Dad. I spent lots of time "with him" while I slept. Funny thing was, I smoked cigarettes in those dreams too. I'd laugh the next morning and thank God for giving me a delightful night chatting with Dad and smoking cigs again! Not sure why that helped so much, but it did. I guess it reminded me that Dad wasn't really dead and gone for good. He was alive in a different place, and I'd see him again. The Healer didn't heal the way I'd been demanding. But He healed, nonetheless, a different kind of wonderful, that's for sure.

The last terrible, wonderful thing that helped grow me while stationed in DC was a ministry opportunity that scared the pants off me (not literally, thank goodness, as I had enough embarrassment as it was!). The church we were going to at the time had a lot of people who worked for the government. Our big Sunday school class included lots of lobbyists, lawyers, and people who worked on the Hill. One Sunday during prayer request time, one of them asked us all to pray about the Freedom of Choice Act[3] that was being voted on soon. He asked us to pray and to specifically ask what God wanted us as individuals to do. Now, being the type of person that does what she's told to do (most of the time), I prayed very sincerely that God would show me. However, I honestly did not think in my heart of hearts that He would ask me to do anything. I felt like it was a fairly safe prayer. I wasn't interested in politics. I had four little kids and rarely even got to watch the nightly news, so I was ignorant. Certainly, a person like me could do nothing in the political arena.

When we got home from church that Sunday, the phone rang. It was a woman I had met at the polls the week prior when I went to vote. The line had been long, so we chatted for a good forty minutes. I didn't recall giving her my contact information, but I must have because she was calling me. She asked if I would come with her to a press conference at the Rayburn Building on Capitol Hill. They were going to interview a gal who had been aborted but miraculously lived. Then there would be all kinds of commentary on the Freedom of Choice Act.

The day of the press conference just happened to be the same day I was supposed to go to Bethesda Naval Hospital in Maryland and have a bone marrow test done because of some weird test results I'd recently received from a checkup. One of the doctors suspected I might have leukemia, so it was no light matter to be tested. Mike was going to take me, as I wouldn't be able to drive afterward. So I thanked the woman from the polls for thinking of me and politely told her no. It did strike me that I'd prayed that prayer and then got a phone call, which would've been something very practical to do, but certainly the Lord understood I was busy.

The next day Mike called from work and asked if I could reschedule my bone marrow procedure, as he had just been ordered to brief the commandant of the marine corps, and you apparently don't tell the commandant you've got other plans. I was able to reschedule it and then realized I would be free to go to that press conference. But I didn't have the woman's contact information, and what would I do with my four kids? The phone rang two more times that day. Once, it was a friend asking me if I could babysit her kids on Friday, and she'd watch all of mine on any other day of the week I would need a sitter. Okay, so I had a sitter, but I didn't know how to get to the Rayburn Building. I had no clue where to go or what to do.

Lord, you've got the wrong girl here.

The second call was from the woman at the polls saying that she thought I might want to change my mind for some reason and come with her, and she would be willing to come and pick me up. I had absolutely no excuses left, so off I went to our nation's capital for a press conference.

It was one of the most exciting things I'd ever really been a part of. It was like a whole different world—smart, sophisticated, well-dressed people gathering and talking about heartfelt issues, seeking to bring about change in a real way. It was so far from my everyday existence of keeping the house clean, cooking, mothering four little ones, and hopefully sneaking some time for a good book (my year of fasting from novels was over).

As it turned out, my new friend was a volunteer lobbyist for a group called Concerned Women for America (CWA), an organization dedicated to impacting the culture for Christ through education and public policy. At the time they had an initiative called 435 (or some number close to that). It was the number of representatives in the House at that time, and the idea was to have a lobbyist for each representative. I think there were only about 150 women lobbyists at the time, but each CWA member was trying to bring in more helpers, hence my friend's persistence in calling me and going out of her way to get me involved. I gladly said yes, as it seemed like such a cool thing to do, and I honestly felt like the Lord had opened a door and was urging me to walk through it. It really was the wildest thing I've ever done because it was so outside my comfort zone. I knew close to nothing about politics. The cool thing was this group was willing and eager to teach us everything we'd need to know.

I started with a basic civics class held in a glorious room down by the Capitol with what appeared to be movers and shakers in this new world I was suddenly plunged into. I hadn't used my brain for much besides Bible study in recent years, so it was very stimulating. Then we were trained in exactly what we would do as lobbyists. We would be assigned a topic that was relevant and given talking points to study and memorize. Then we'd be responsible for making an appointment with whatever congressman we were assigned to.

Thankfully, they paired us up, and one person did all the talking, and the other person just prayed silently through the whole meeting. I doubt I would have had the courage to do it if I hadn't been the silent praying person the first couple of months. The month I was assigned to be the talker instead of the prayer, I was absolutely petrified. The subject was homosexuals in the military. I studied like a maniac and had all the facts and talking points memorized. I was shaking like a leaf when we walked into the Canon Office Building, went through security, and into the congressman's office.

We were waiting to meet with the aide assigned to us when a group of protestors from the gay rights parade that was taking place that week walked into the office. One guy singled me out, as I had a "Stop FOCA" button on. Two separate issues, of course (FOCA stood for Freedom of Choice Act), but this guy got in my face and started saying I was the kind of person that hated him and his kind of people. I was so shocked. I hate controversy of any kind. I'm not a debater, I'm a people pleaser. I felt sick to my stomach. My prayer partner must have been powerfully inter-ceding because I responded with what I think was grace and said, "I don't hate you at all, nor do I hate your kind of people. Jesus never hated people. He loved them. He just hated the brokenness this world brings."

I think he liked the first part of what I said, but the second part inflamed him. He said I needed to realize that they have no choice in being given same-sex desires, so I was ignorant to call it broken-ness. It defined him. I told him I very respectfully disagreed, as we are made in God's image for His purposes, and that's what defines all of us. (Little did I realize at the time that I'd have this very same conversation with my precious daughter, Molly, who feels like her same-sex attraction defines her and keeps her from God. But I'm getting ahead of the story.)

Thankfully, the congressional aide assigned to meet with us ap-peared at that point, and I didn't have to continue. The man was so hostile, and I was already nervous before he started yelling at me; now I was a complete wreck. I whispered to my prayer partner that I couldn't remember any of the talking points, and maybe she should take over and I would just pray. She looked at me like I was nuts. I realized she was horrified that I was choking at the last minute here. She wasn't prepared, and this was a very dicey conversation we were about to have. I silently screamed, *Jesus, you have to help me. Now!*

We sat down in the aide's office, and although this will sound dramatic to you, I have to tell it like it happened. As soon as I opened my mouth, my heart stopped pounding, my hands stopped shaking, my stomach stopped clenching, and I was perfectly calm. Words flowed out of my mouth that sounded good and rational. It was almost like an out-of-body experience where I was watching myself have a great conversation with this man in a powerful position.

At the end of our appointment time, the aide actually said he enjoyed talking to us, and we'd given him food for thought. Now, I realize politicians have to be suave and soothing to their constituents, but I felt he was being sincere.

I was absolutely elated! I'd never really felt the power of the Holy Spirit at work in and through me in such an indisputable way before. Now, the elation wasn't due to my thinking that we'd win the day with our arguments. It truly was because God had called me to speak up, recognize that my voice had value, and understand our system of democracy where the individual has the right to be heard and represented, and then He gave me the courage to go do something. The actual results were not for me to worry about. I'd done my part.

The culmination of this particular ministry was when I realized that my main task was to recruit others to be lobbyists, as we were moving again shortly and I wouldn't be able to do it myself anymore.

The Precept Bible Study I taught had grown huge, so in just telling my experiences to that crowd, many came forward and asked how they could get involved. By the time I left, I was replaced with nearly twenty others that would represent the voice of Christ well to our nation's leaders. Writing about this today, after all the political unrest and crowds of people storming the Capitol "in the name of Christ," makes me uneasy. All kinds of violent acts have been rationalized this way; I think of the Crusades as an example. *Really? Christ told you to storm the Capitol and kill people and try to overturn an election with violence?* One of my brothers vehemently said he didn't think evangelicals should ever be allowed to have a part in politics. I understood his anger, but of course I disagreed. This country was founded on the premise that all men are created equal, that they are endowed by their Creator with certain unalienable rights, that among these are life, liberty, and the pursuit of happiness. Evangelicals have a right to be heard just as Catholics and Jews and Muslims and atheists do. But we all have a responsibility to voice our concerns respectfully as law-abiding citizens.

I actually think those waving "Jesus Saves" signs have a higher accountability to act with patience and kindness, not bearing a grudge, not being easily angered or demanding their own way. Because if Jesus saved them, it was to make them like Him. And He is love, and that's how love acts. Again, I digress from the story. Jesus saved me and called me and equipped me and led me to be a very small part in a ministry that stretched me. I learned so much and felt His presence and help in a real way.

The terrible, wonderful things that happened during this season of my life made the opening verses in the book of James come alive for me: "Consider it all joy when you encounter various trials, knowing that the testing of your faith produces endurance, and let endurance have it's perfect result, so that you might be perfect and complete, lacking in nothing" (James 1:2–4). God really does use various trials for good in the lives of His children. He uses marriage difficulties, horrible illnesses of loved ones, and difficult job assignments to stretch and grow our faith that we might be more and more conformed to the image of His Son. Once I realized that the good God brings out of bad stuff is not a reversal of the situation but a reformation of my inner being, I could rejoice.

Sagebrush Terrace, Twentynine Palms, California

CHAPTER 8

Finding Streams
in the Desert

*Holy Spirit, I'm so grieved I have to leave
the excitement of DC and live in a
barren desert for the next three years.
Can you breathe hope into me
that I'll survive and thrive out there
and not sink too deeply into self-pity?*

Early in our marriage we visited Mike's parents, who were stationed in Redlands, California. My father-in-law was a chaplain in the air force at the time, and they lived only a couple of hours away from Edwards Air Force Base, where Mike had gone to high school. So he wanted to visit Edwards for old times' sake and show me around. It's located in the northwestern corner of the Mojave Desert. After the tour I told my dear husband that I'd follow him anywhere the military sent us except the desert. I'm fond of trees, grass, and water, and I saw very little of that at Edwards. It seemed so barren, lonely, hot, desolate, and brown. Although I'd made myself clear about never moving to a desert, the marine corps chose to ignore me. Mike came home with orders to Twentynine Palms, located right in the middle of the Mojave Desert. *Ugh!*

I begged him to get those orders changed, as I didn't know

what I'd done to be punished with a "desert experience." I couldn't see us going from a thriving metropolis like Washington, DC, to a base where the nearest big store was a Walmart forty-five minutes away in Yucca Valley. The kids and I had gone to downtown DC almost once a week for what we called adventure day and had seen every Smithsonian museum and monument in a lavishly casual way as we had time. We'd had all kinds of restaurants and malls and theaters and culture at our fingertips for three years, and now we were headed for Nothingsville. Oh my, did I feel sorry for myself.

As usual, God had a plan for me that was beyond my idea of comfort and the good life. A friend gave me a beautiful little book as a going-away present called *Streams in the Desert* by Lettie Cowan.[1] I thought it was just meant to be kind of funny, as she knew how horrified I was at the thought of moving off to a dry and thirsty land. But it actually was a huge source of comfort and wisdom as I read the daily devotionals.

We moved into another cul-de-sac and once more had neighbors that became family. Our next-door neighbors were the O'Neals, and down the street lived the Bowlings. We became tight immediately, and our kids bonded quickly. That helped with the lonely pangs of being separated from my tribe in Virginia. We walked together every morning, went to wives' gatherings, and had dinner parties with the hubbies and picnics with all our kids. I quickly discovered it's not the offerings of an environment that makes a place special—it's the people you get to know and the good works that God prepared beforehand that you should walk in. God had plans!

There were two chapels on this base—one for Protestants, and across a big expanse of grass (yes, actual grass that was watered constantly) was one for Catholics. My new neighbor and walking buddy was Irish Catholic and had grown up in Chicago. We had so much in common, and I really enjoyed her company, so I invited her to come to this women's Bible study I was going to join. When she stated she couldn't go to a Protestant Women of the Chapel Bible study because she was Catholic, I immediately understood the problem.

I went to our head chaplain and asked if we could rename our women's Bible study so it would be all inclusive. Good thing I'd had a course in politics back in DC! This was no easy task. I had to write bylaws for the new organization. I had to meet with the Catholic chaplain, who wasn't really eager to give his support, as he thought I'd try to convert his women. I assured him we would just study Scripture and try to keep denominational differences at bay. We could choose to agree on the essentials and agree to disagree on the nonessentials.

He went straight to John 3 and asked what I would say about Jesus telling Nicodemus he had to be born again. I told him my interpretation, which wasn't the same as his. That made him uncomfortable, but I kept appealing to the idea of encouraging people to seek God and learn His Word, not just spoon-feed people for fear they might think differently than you wish they would. Couldn't people be trusted to talk to God themselves about what they were reading? Couldn't God be trusted to help them understand? He finally reluctantly said okay; he wouldn't ban any Catholic women from studying with us, but he wouldn't advertise it either.

We kicked off a group we called Christian Women's Fellowship, or CWF. The head chaplain was good to us. He gave us money and a little office and helped us order materials and advertise. Word spread that we were doing fun and meaningful things and it was open to all: officers and enlisted wives, Protestant and Catholic, Jewish, atheist, Muslim . . . whatever! Come! We had all kinds of outreach activities like the Beauty in You night. We had hair stylists, makeup artists, nail technicians, accessory people, and all that kind of thing for women to get makeovers. Then, the heart of the night was a talk about inner beauty: all the outward stuff in the world is fine and can be fun, but what will really make you stunning is the light that can shine from your eyes, the love that can be embodied in your actions, the kindness and grace that can flow from your mouth—all through being in love with Jesus.

We had retreats and studies and brought in professional speakers. We took trips to concerts (like Michael W. Smith) and conferences. It turned out to be an incredible time of getting to watch women come alive in Christ. The isolation of the base was a blessing, not a curse. Nothingsville proved to be a great place to concentrate on spiritual things because there was a severe lack of worldly distractions. We all realized that God was at work out there in the Mojave Desert, and we were so privileged to be invited into that work and empowered to make His name known.

What got started there in the nineties has strengthened and grown through the years. My son, Matt, and his wife, Jill, and three of my precious grandbabies are stationed out in Twentynine Palms as I write this. Jill attends CWF along with approximately eighty other women in the day group and forty more who come at night. A good friend of mine was the president last year, and she told me how the group continues to help women come alive spiritually and then grow in the grace and knowledge of our Lord and Savior.

I had no idea why God thought I needed a desert experience in my life, but I am glad in retrospect that He dragged me there. The terrain is a bit like some of the places in Israel where Jesus ministered, and it really wasn't lonely and desolate and barren like I thought it would be. Brown and hot, yes! But brown turned out to have a beauty of its own. One of the kids asked why everything looked like toast. I laughed at that description, but on our way out of town, off to our next duty station, I admitted how much I loved toast. Those were great years of learning to do ministry outside of a denominational church. I felt like we'd really had an Acts early church experience when I sat beside my Catholic and Jewish and charismatic and Southern Baptist and Northern Presbyterian and Black and White and Korean and Hispanic and enlisted and officers' wives and oh, so many more friends who had perhaps been separated before but had now become sisters, and we collectively worshiped our one God, one Lord, one Savior, hallelujah!

House near the Awase Meadows Golf Course,
Okinawa, Japan

CHAPTER 9

Navigating a Foreign Land

*Jesus, I guess it goes without saying that
I'm going to need your help in this next season.
Mike is stationed with the navy and
will be gone most of our time on the island.
This is a long way from Wisconsin, Lord.
Help me navigate my way, fit in,
and love the people of our host nation well.*

I'd always wanted to live overseas, but what I had in mind was Europe. I wanted to ski in the Alps and shop in the Bavarian markets and drink wine in Paris. I had met army friends in the past who lived in Germany but then spent weekends and vacations seeing all of Europe. And I longed for that. Unfortunately, marine tankers don't get to go to Europe very often, so our overseas tour ended up being Okinawa, Japan. Now, I was down for that because people were telling me it was the Hawaiian Islands of the East. But navigating a new duty station without knowing the language or the rules was a lot trickier and scarier than I realized. I thought we would just live on base, and it would be like living on the island of Cuba, where you are in a foreign country but in a little American enclave. Problem was, we were not assigned base housing for various reasons and had to find something on the economy.

We found a cool house that was completely unlike anything we'd ever lived in. It had tatami floor mats in many of the rooms. Many of the inside walls were paper screens that you could slide open or close to create closed-off space or bigger areas. The bathrooms had urinals, which I thought was odd and kind of gross, but the boys loved that feature. It didn't have an oven, just kind of a hot plate set up in the kitchen. And if we used our microwave and the hot plate at the same time, the fuses blew. There was a door in the floor of the kitchen that opened to a storage space. Apparently that was for your vegetables or potatoes or whatever. It was kind of nice having an excuse to not cook much.

There was a gorgeous winding staircase made of some kind of polished wood that gleamed, and the landing was wide with deep windows overlooking the jungle outside. The house was somewhat on a hill but surrounded on three sides by jungle. No lawn. The stairs led to two bedrooms and an attic with a huge chain and padlock on the door. Somehow the kids got the impression that scary things were locked behind that door, so getting the kids tucked in at night was a bit challenging. The boys' bedroom had a balcony with a view of the East China Sea. I thought that was cool; they worried someone could climb up to the balcony and come in the door and get them.

We developed a beautiful routine for bedtime that I still think about today. I'd sit on the side of the bottom bunk where John slept, Matt on the top bunk, and Mike on a futon on the floor. We were only allowed to bring so much furniture. The rest you rented from the navy. So initially we had one set of bunk beds and then mattresses on the tatami mats downstairs for the master bedroom. Molly slept with me for months till our household goods came. Then she had our queen-sized bed in the other upstairs room, but she was too scared to sleep in there alone. Poor Mike got elected to leave the futon and sleep with Molly. It was roomy and comfortable, but in retrospect, I think it was embarrassing for him, and of course, his brothers teased him mercilessly about it all. Anyway, the routine we developed was wonderful. After we prayed, I would sing the song "I Cast All My Cares upon You."[1]

The lyrics are based on the verse in 1 Peter that says, "Cast all your anxiety on Him because He cares for you." It talks about laying all your burdens down, and the melody is lilting and sweet somehow.

I mention this because I had to sing this song to myself a whole lot in the year we spent on this beautiful island. Like Monterey, the environment was gorgeous but also had a dark side, specifically, typhoons! We had just moved in and been given navy furniture. Our own household goods wouldn't arrive for another couple of months. So the place was quite bare, but did I mention there was a tree in the living room, right next to the ancestral altar? And when the moving crew came to give us the navy furniture, they all bowed to the tree every time they came in our front door. I wasn't sure what was happening, as none of them spoke English, but it was obvious there was some kind of idol worship going on with that tree and altar. We went to the exchange and bought a TV, and I always felt guilty that we set it up right on that altar. The ugly Americans had arrived! But it really was the only place for it. We ended up not watching TV all that much because we only got one channel, some military-run channel that constantly repeated ads like, "It's important to stay hydrated on Okinawa." That got old quick.

Right after we moved in, Mike had to leave for an exercise on a navy ship for a month. And a typhoon hit the island. The kids and I huddled in this somewhat bare house with trees and urinals, and the wind and rain lashed the house and trees of the jungle, leaving green slime all over the windows. It was very scary. I had to cast my cares on God big-time!

He sent a beautiful friend to our rescue. One of my best friends from Twentynine Palms lived on one of the bases there in a beautiful home. She invited the kids and me to stay with them the whole week as the typhoon worsened and left streets and stores closed. We actually ended up having the time of our life with that family as they had tons of good food, movies, games, delicious bottles of wine, and glorious conversation! We really were kind of sad when the typhoon ended and we had to go back to reality.

Going back immediately involved me standing in the small clearing between our Japanese house and the jungle, scraping green slime off everything. I kept picturing snakes and spiders and other animals and reptiles slithering out of the jungle and attacking me while my back was turned. We'd already encountered geckos living in our bathrooms, scaling the walls as you tried to do your business. I learned to live with those, but the huge spiders and snakes were untenable.

Mold was a constant problem, as was rust—problems we never envisioned. We had brought our lawn mower, not knowing we wouldn't have a lawn or a garage. So it sat in our carport area and rusted out completely. Mike's suits were in a small cupboard in the tatami-covered room we used as our bedroom. They'd been crunched in there for months when he finally went to put one on, and it was full of mold. We had to pretty much get rid of everything he owned (not really a great loss, as he didn't have a lot of civilian clothes at the time). The kids had brought roller hockey gear, and when they stuck their fingers in the big gloves, they came out green and sticky, as the mold had got inside somehow. Out those went! We did have room air conditioners that might have helped, but the bill for running them was humongous, so we just slid open the big sliding windows and tried for breezes wafting through to cool us off. Coming from the arid desert heat to the thick, swampy, humid heat of Okinawa was a bit of a shock to the system.

The next issue I had to cast on the Lord because I didn't know what to do was paying the bills. That first month these slips of paper with Japanese writing started appearing under my front door. Our landlord lived in a teeny-tiny apartment near us, so I knocked on his door for help, but he spoke no English. I spoke no Japanese. Not helpful. I finally drove over to the rental agency we'd used to find the place. They told me these were all bills I needed to pay. How and where and how much, and could I use American money? The how was various places. Water bill at the gas station convenience store down the street, electric at a bank, and rent at the rental agency. No American money accepted. I felt the Lord's presence and His prompting. *Use your common sense, Katie! This can't be that hard!* Okay, get money exchanged, hand over various bills at the various places, and just hold out wads of the money and pantomime take what you need to cover this. It worked. And I'm pretty sure I didn't get ripped off.

We acclimated and adjusted to all the quirks of living in a foreign country and truly enjoyed the beaches and the lavish parks. Since no one has much of a yard, the parks are huge and equipped with lots of picturesque bridges and landscaping and equipment to rent and treats to consume. But right when life started feeling comfortable, everything changed.

Our original orders were for a two-year tour, and we were just shy of completing one. I'd joined a cultural exchange program and had made some beautiful Japanese friends. I was learning to love sushi and tempura and could somewhat handle chopsticks. We had all kinds of fun trips planned for the next year. I was scheduled to go to Korea with friends, all of us were going to Australia for the Christmas vacation, and my mom and uncle and aunt were coming for a visit. I was so eager to more fully explore the island with them. I'd saved all kinds of touristy things to do for when they arrived. Oh, the best-laid plans of mice and men! None of it was to come about.

Mike was gone again when I got a phone call from the States at 2:00 one morning. I distinctly remember the time, as it caused my heart to beat out of control. I was sure something had happened to Mike. Mike was fine, but something was going to happen that was both exciting and stress inducing. The guy on the phone was from Headquarters Marine Corps, and he told me Mike had been selected to be the next commanding officer of the tank battalion in Twentynine Palms, and they needed us to pack up quickly and report there within the month.

This was before cell phones and email and such. Mike was off in Thailand on some exercise, so there was no easy way to communicate with him. If he found a pay phone somewhere, he could call or use one of the military lines, but that was always complicated. I had no way to contact him—except of course through prayer. I started telling God to tell Mike to phone home! And he did, thank God, the next night.

This assignment came out of the blue. Someone else was slated to be the CO. Apparently he'd been caught having an affair with an enlisted guy's wife. He was going to be court-martialed. It all happened suddenly, and Mike was then handpicked to take this guy's place. Now, the stressful part of all this was Mike wasn't due back from Thailand for a couple more weeks, so I'd have to arrange the move, sell the cars, contact the schools to pull the kids out, and other such details on my own.

I actually only had one car to sell because I'd just totaled our second one in a scary accident. Driving was a real challenge over there as it's all on the "wrong" side, and there aren't clearly defined traffic lanes and parking and such. We were warned that if we got in an accident, it would be our fault, and with the anti-American sentiment going on in those days, they might very well choose to prosecute you. We had all heard the nightmare story of the wife of a marine who'd been jailed for hitting a pedestrian. I was taking the kids to school when I was broadsided by a small sports car that I couldn't see coming because of all the parked cars along the roadway. It was pouring rain, so that didn't help. The guy who hit me didn't speak English. Neither did the police when they arrived. Why would they? I was in Japan, and it was my bad for not learning their language. I tried but failed miserably. I told the kids to take the umbrella and walk home. Unknown to me, the boys told Molly that I was going to jail and she probably wouldn't see me again. So mean! I probably should have kept them all with me as I tried to figure out what I was supposed to do, but I thought I might be there for hours. Again, no cell phones or any way to get help from a friend or a translator.

Once more, my only source of help was the Divine! I begged Him to intervene here and help me out. After pantomiming with the police for a bit, I got the impression I could just walk away. The guy who hit me didn't seem angry or accusatory of me. I guessed they would call a tow truck somehow, and that was it. I gathered all the junk out of the trunk and walked back home in the rain. I did call the legal office on base and explained what had happened, and they said I'd know sooner or later if I was in trouble. *Okay . . .*

Now, a couple of days later, I was hearing we were leaving the island shortly. I was sad about missing out on glorious trips, but part of me was relieved that I might get out of town before my driving crime got me in trouble! Thank You, Jesus, for all the weird twists and turns life takes. Once more, life wasn't going like I'd planned, but I was learning to trust His ways and His purposes. The move came together quickly, and we were on a plane and headed back to California.

Ashurst Street, Twentynine Palms,
California (Again!)

CHAPTER 10

Applying the Golden Rule

*You've called Mike to be the commanding officer
of a tank battalion back in California, so
I'm now the CO's wife with expectations on me
to lead the wives and spearhead family activities.
Lord, the problem is most of the wives won't speak to me,
as they wanted a different CO-wife combo chosen.
I need some hope in this dire situation.
How can I lead if no one wants to follow?*

You'd think arriving back on American soil would make life easy breezy in comparison to navigating a foreign culture, but I think Jesus meant it when He said, "In this world you will have trouble." We hadn't even settled into our new house all the way when two of my sons got in a wrestling match that ended with a broken bone. Mike had just taken his new battalion out for training in the desert, so as far as I knew, he couldn't be reached. I told the ER staff it didn't matter; I'd handle it without him. The surgeon decided differently when he couldn't get Matt's arm bone snapped back into the correct position and was going to have to operate. In came Mike after being summoned by the powers that be, his gun and holster still strapped across his chest. He looked so incongruent with his tired, rough-looking face and Nomex uniform (like a jumpsuit—think Tom Cruise in *Top Gun*) among the sterile cleanliness of the hospital. I truly was glad to have him, though, as one of us could stay with Matt and the other could go home and be with the other three kids.

God truly did a miracle as we waited and prayed. The surgeon came out unexpectedly early and said he'd felt an overwhelming urge before he cut Matt to yank on the arm one more time, and the bone slid easily into place. He was amazed. I was too and so very thankful for the healing power of Jesus on display.

Matt visited the ER three more times that year. Once a hockey puck landed smack hard between his nose and mouth. One inch higher or lower, and he'd have lost all his teeth or smashed his nose in. And once his lip got caught on a chain basketball net as he went up for a layup and ripped open on the way down. And again when he broke his collarbone playing football in PE. Needless to say, the ER staff started eyeing us warily as possibly abusive parents. It was not a comfortable feeling.

Broken bones and lips are one thing, broken relationships another. I was very excited to jump into the tank battalion's wives group. A friend told me her husband had been on the board that had decided to offer Mike the command. It was stated that if they brought Hawkins on board, they'd be getting two for the price of one because I had been an active participant in the wives groups of the last two battalions Mike had served in. They believed I could add some value in raising the morale of the marines and their families. I was eager to do just that. I wanted to be a witness to the light and hope and joy all could have through Jesus.

Well, I got off to a very bad start. I kept waiting for the outgoing executive officer's wife to contact me. It was protocol for the senior wife to hold a coffee to welcome the incoming wife and introduce her around. No invite came. No phone calls even. Not a word of welcome. There was a hail and farewell party we were to attend, where the outgoing crew would be recognized and the incoming welcomed, so I figured I'd meet everyone at that event. Problem was, no one wanted to talk to me. It's hard to meet people when they are sitting close around a table and won't rise to greet you or invite you to have a seat. I have never felt so awkward in all my life. It turned out that some of the wives felt the outgoing executive officer (XO) should have been given the command instead of Mike, so they gathered around his wife and didn't feel obligated to welcome me. I'd heard tales of officers' wives being less than gracious to others for power play reasons, but I'd never personally experienced it. What could I do but pray for the softening of hearts and some open doors?

The God who told us clearly that loving one another was the important thing did just that. Thankfully, there were a couple of clearheaded gals in the group who realized that I had nothing to do with the supposed injustice and decided to press on with the reality of me. I threw my own welcome coffee, and they got some of the other wives to come. We ended up having a good time, and word spread that I wasn't snooty or rejoicing in the old CO's downfall and not bad-mouthing the XO's wife.

Mike and I planned a party for the officers, which turned out well, and then another one for the whole battalion and their kids (with help from the battalion staff, as there were over seven hundred men assigned to the tank battalion, so it was a huge event.) Mike had always been a beloved leader, as he is kind and considerate. He's also extremely knowledgeable and a hard worker. He's handsome and athletic but very humble. I don't think I'm just saying this as a prejudiced wife, but I'll risk that being the case and say it anyway.

Mike won the respect of the men in his battalion, and that was a huge factor in the wives softening to me. By the Marine Corps

Ball in October of that year, we were a solid little unit of friends. This might sound sexist or weird, but we became known on the base as the "Tanker Babes." We had these little tank charms made, and we all wore them. Others wanted to be honorary members because they saw how much fun we had together, how we supported one another, and how all the petty politicking and backbiting that can be common in some wives groups had been firmly set aside. I like to think of the whole experience as proof that Jesus sends very real help and hope in seemingly difficult situations.

The beautiful ending to the whole couple of years was one only He could have brought about. When our tour of duty was up, the new incoming CO turned out to be the old XO along with, of course, his wife, who'd snubbed me. Some of the gals who had been around when we arrived and witnessed the less-than-stellar welcome wondered how I'd now treat her. I invoked the Golden Rule and said, "We will go above and beyond to make her feel welcome. Treat others as you wish to be treated, not as you have been treated."

Some saw my behavior as killing her with kindness, and there might have been some truth in that. I always have to apologize to the Lord when my motives are not as pure as I want them to be!

We rolled out the red carpet for her with flowers and coffees and gifts and meals and such. A couple days before we left town, she and her husband had Mike and me over for dinner. She apologized for the way she'd treated me and was so grateful for the kindness shown her. I knew that Jesus had just put the capstone on this odd season of leadership, showing me that when we act like Him, with love and grace and mercy and genuine humility toward others, it brings unity and harmony and resolution.

Ending well is a joyous feeling, and I was happy as we left the dry desert for the well-watered New England town of Newport,

Rhode Island. The only dark cloud on the horizon was that we'd got news that my sister, Sheila, had cancer. Well, I personally knew someone who could heal! I'd seen Him heal my mom physically and my dad spiritually. I'd seen Him heal marriages and friendships and, just recently, bring wholeness to a group of people. I was sure He'd do something miraculous again. Off we went across the country for a whole new adventure.

Jackson Road, Fort Adams,
Newport, Rhode Island

CHAPTER 11

Finding Help
in a Sewing Circle

Lord, now my sister is dying of cancer?
She lives in Tennessee,
and I'm newly ensconced in Rhode Island.
Can you help me help her somehow
despite not being there in person for her?
Would you heal her?

We stopped in Knoxville, Tennessee, on our way across country. My extended family met us there at a huge mountain chalet in the Smoky Mountains, which we all chipped in and rented. It had four levels, two hot tubs, twelve bedrooms, two huge sitting rooms with fireplaces, a game room, and views that were spectacular. It was ideal for the perfect family reunion. We had such a great time, but looking back now after experiencing cancer myself, I realize how awful my sister, Sheila, must have felt. She put on a good game face, and we took our cues from her. We talked and laughed, went hiking, played cards and games, soaked in the giant hot tubs together, and shared our lives. Every one of us had very high hopes that Sheila would beat this cancer and we would have many more years together for reunions like this. We were wrong.

Shortly after the reunion, we arrived in Newport, Rhode Island, a seaside city on the southern tip of Aquidneck Island. Island living again! I really do prefer islands and oceans over deserts and mountains, but they each have their unique beauty. I loved our housing area located on Fort Adams, an old army fort situated on a peninsula and turned into a state park. The Eisenhower Summer White House was a mansion you drove by as you came and went from the area. Jackie Bouvier Kennedy's house, Hammersmith Farm, was right down the street. Standing on the patio where she and Jack stood during their wedding reception was incredible. There was so much to see and do in this little town so alive with festivals and mansions and historical markers and one of the most famous walking paths in the world, the Cliff Walk.

But I had a heaviness of heart amid the joy and excitement of our new place. I told God that I was not going to get involved in anything until He made it very clear what I was to do. My usual MO was to dive right in and just assume I should start a Bible study or join this group or do this or that, but this time I felt a halt in my spirit and the necessity to surrender all my usual control to wait upon the Lord's direction. Funny how quickly it came and how out of the ordinary it was.

We hadn't even unpacked yet when a family who was moving out of our housing area invited us over for dinner. They started telling us all the fun things to do in Newport. The wife told me about a quilting group she had joined and assured me I would want to do it also. She showed me all the things she'd made, and of course I oohed and aahed, but inside I was thinking, *That is the last thing I would ever join!* I don't sew. I don't even mend. If something gets ripped in our house, either Mike fixes it or we get rid of it and just buy a new article. I wouldn't even consider taking a quilting class and sewing for fun.

But the wife explained that there would be a welcome and sign-up coffee in a gorgeous community center overlooking Narragansett Bay, and you could see all the different groups and tours offered and sign up for things. I made sure we went to that but with no intention of going anywhere near the quilt group table. However, Mike visited that table and came to me and said, "Honey, I think you should join this quilting group."

I said, "Are you crazy? I don't have a sewing machine, and I don't sew, and I don't like to sew. So why would I do that?"

He said, "Maybe you'd learn, and maybe you'd like it."

I assured him I wouldn't and visited other tables. Then a friend I had been stationed with in Twentynine Palms came up to me all excited and asked if I'd seen there was a quilting group that we could join. I was again adamant, telling her, "I don't sew." She assured me that she would help me, I could use her machine, and that we really could have a good time doing this together. It finally dawned on me that just possibly this could be God nudging me toward something He wanted me to do. So I put my name on the sign-up sheet and decided that the least I could do was go to the first meeting and check it out.

I sat there while the leader talked about sampler quilts and fat quarters and bias and tension and all sorts of foreign words that made no sense to me. Quilting is a whole world with its own language. The only thing I did understand was the assignment to go shopping and pick out six different materials that complemented each other. I still wasn't sure this was God-led, so I made a deal with Him. *If this is one of those good works You want me to do for some odd reason, then let me find material I absolutely love. And if I can't find anything that really excites me, then I'm off the hook. I mean, there is so much to do here in Newport, and I don't want to waste my time!*

I walked into a fabric shop, and there was a display right near the front door that was absolutely gorgeous. One of the fabrics had all these country-looking angels on it. And I say country because I don't want you to think Rembrandt's angels or wispy, white-winged creatures. Do you remember Debbie Mum as a designer back in the nineties? It was her stuff. Cute, fat angels, and the colors were striking greens and maroons and golds, and there were six different choices that coordinated, and I could visualize how pretty it would all look together. So I surrendered to the idea, bought it all, and proceeded to try to learn how to make a new square every week. Apparently that's what a sampler quilt is. You make a bunch of different squares, and then at some point sew them all together, and you have a quilt. Well, there are a few more steps, but that's basically it.

Probably needless to say, but I'll say it anyway. My squares were horrible. Even with my friend helping me, I couldn't sew a straight line, my corners never matched up, and it was truly a debacle! I could tell the other quilters were wondering what I was doing in this group. I mean, it was clear to everyone that this was not something I was good at. I wasn't even mediocre—I was terrible! We had been together about a month, and I had four super-ugly squares done when I flew down to Tennessee to visit my sister.

Sheila was to have a second-look surgery to see if the chemotherapy she'd been on all summer had been effective. My mother flew in from Wisconsin, my other sister from California, and we were all very positive and convinced that Sheila would be fine. We were playing bridge in the lobby of the hospital and anticipating a long wait when a doctor suddenly came out and summoned us. He said they didn't even need to do the surgery because it was clearly evident that the cancer had spread everywhere, and there was no hope. We were completely shocked. After many tears and conversations, my sister and her husband decided to keep fighting at all costs. I was devastated and felt so very helpless.

On the plane ride home, I poured out my heart to God. I asked Him to show me what I could do for Sheila. And He answered, *Make a quilt.*

It hit me like a ton of bricks. A person who's going to be sick for a while might need a nice blanket. Especially a blanket with angels on it! It could be a symbol of hope and love and a reminder that this life isn't all there is. So I went back to the quilting group and asked the leader if I could address everyone. I told the ladies that before coming to Rhode Island, I had asked God to show me clearly what He would have me involve myself in. When I felt Him nudge me toward a quilting class, I doubted that I'd heard Him right.

They all laughed when I showed them my squares once more and explained that I really wondered if I was where I needed to be; was I using my time wisely? Until I got the news that Sheila was dying. Then it all became very clear. I told them that I was going to visit my sister again in a month, and I would love to have the quilt finished by then. But I was going to need their help. I asked if each woman would be willing to make one of the squares, and then we could all piece it together. Everybody jumped on board.

Now I know some of them thought I was a little odd refer-ring to God leading me. But all of them made a square, and when we stitched them together and had the top done, they all agreed to gather around it and offer up prayers. It was so beautiful, as I knew a couple of the ladies were Jewish, some Catholic, others Protestant, at least one agnostic—and yet at a time of desperation at the near death of a loved one, all had a reverence and yearning to connect with a higher power. That prayer time, meant to bless my sister, blessed all of us. We started a Bible study in that same community center where we quilted, and some of those ladies came to it. And that was just one small part of God's beautiful plan.

When I took the finished quilt down to Sheila and gave it to her, she just stared at it and then looked at me and said, "You don't sew! What is this?"

So I told her the whole story and then added something like "It might not look like God is answering our prayers. It might seem like He doesn't care about you and your suffering, but I feel like this quilt is proof that He does. When a group of relative strangers get together and sew beautiful angels together for someone they don't know just to bring some comfort and hope, there is a good and holy force behind that! And it's God! He wants you to know Him and trust Him even as you walk through the valley of the shadow of death."

I still felt like He was going to deliver a miracle and heal her. She went through countless operations trying to cut out various tumors and open up blockages. Each time she took her angel blanket to the hospital with her. She said doctors, nurses, aides that passed by them in the hallway, and visitors, would all comment, "Oh, look at the angels with you!"

One night Sheila told me that her husband and kids had gone home and she was all alone, facing yet another surgery the next day. A terrible, gripping fear came over her, and she was shaking, but when she looked down at the quilt covering her, the thought came that she wasn't alone—God was with her and loved her. A peace entered the room that was as overwhelming as the fear had been.

That was all I needed to hear to look back on my plea for help from God. He had given her something tangible to communicate His love for her and presence with her at a crucial time. We draped the quilt over her coffin. God was glorified as we told the story over and over of its making. He chose not to heal her physically, but she made her peace with Him spiritually before she left this world. She joined Dad.

I'm so grateful for the nudging supplied by the Holy Spirit through an acquaintance, a friend, and my husband to open my eyes to the real help God wanted to send through a circle of women making quilts, of all things. If I had brushed it off as not making sense, my helplessness in the face of Sheila's cancer season and ultimate death would have been debilitating. Having something to work on, something that brought some comfort to my precious sister, some tangible reassurance of God's presence as we all walked through the valley of death with her was such a good gift.

I would desperately need the joy and peace that only the Lord, the generous gift giver, can bring to a troubled soul for the next season of grief and challenges. We had to leave the beautiful peninsula of Fort Adams and venture on to Washington, DC, where Mike would work on the Joint Chiefs of Staff at the Pentagon.

Westchester Court, Stafford, Virginia

CHAPTER 12

Walking an Explosive Road

*Lord, we've survived a major hurricane blowing through,
snipers on the loose killing people randomly in our
area, and the horrors of 9/11.
All four of my kids are teenagers, and I think I'm
blowing it in the parenting department, as Molly has
an eating disorder and the boys have gone a bit wild.
Can you send some hope?*

Moving to the DC area once again, albeit farther south this time, was like getting in the fast lane on I-95 and staying there. Crazy things came upon us along with all the regular ups and downs of life. On September 11, 2001, terrorists attacked the Pentagon. Mike was working there, as was his brother, Jim. I was in a staff meeting at church when we heard the news.

Between the time of the attacks on the World Trade Center at 8:46 a.m. and 9:03 a.m. and the Flight 93 crash at 10:03 a.m., radio transmissions alerted that American Airlines Flight 77 was headed toward the White House. This was the plane that crashed into the western facade of the Pentagon at 9:37 a.m. (Timeline gathered from various news stories on the internet.)

One gal in our staff meeting started panicking, as her husband was at the Pentagon that day for a meeting. Dizziness swept over me, and my stomach clenched, but a supernatural calmness came over my spirit. I said out loud, without really thinking about it, so I know it was Spirit led, "Well, isn't this where the rubber meets the road? We preach about trusting God. Should we now practice what we preach? Let's pray."

We all got on our knees and prayed and then got up and found a little portable TV and set it up in our office area so we could monitor the news. Phone lines to the Pentagon were out or overloaded, so trying to call anyone to see if our husbands were alive was fruitless. Thankfully, my brother-in-law was a general in the air force, so he had access to some kind of phone that worked, and his secretary called me to let me know both Mike and he were safe. My poor friend spent the whole day and most of the night knowing nothing about her own husband's well-being.

The schools were pulling all the military kids out of classes and telling them what had happened. They were allowed to go home early if they desired, so I went and picked up my kids. My son Mike was a freshman in college, and I couldn't get through to him, so he also spent the day wondering if his loved ones were alive.

We didn't see big Mike for days after the attack, as he was ordered to the secret bunker in Pennsylvania. His office hadn't been hit directly but was so filled with smoke they couldn't operate. He worked for a team that had been tracking Osama bin Laden. The workload had just become more vitally important. Mike's boss took a helicopter to the bunker but for some reason ordered Mike to drive. The traffic around the area was insane, as you can imagine. It took him forever to get there. The next months were extremely hard for him. He worked nonstop.

It was unsettling for our family too. Mike had been deployed before, so having him gone was nothing new, but for some reason his brush with death and the tension our whole nation was feeling just put a new pressure on us all. Mike had been at a meeting in Henderson Hall, which is up the hill from the Pentagon, when the plane hit. He heard about the attack when someone ran in and shouted, "The Pentagon is under attack!" An eerie silence fell for seconds, then everyone in the big lecture hall jumped up and ran down the hill into the controlled chaos. They all had what is called muster spots preassigned for any such emergencies.

Fears and grueling schedules finally seemed to settle down till the next fall brought a sniper attack to our area, which was so creepy. The shooters seemed to just randomly pick targets, killing ten people and injuring three during a three-week period in October. Daily life was seriously interrupted. One victim was gunned down getting gas, making that routine chore a cause for anxiety. Another was shot going into Michaels, a favorite craft store in town. Now shopping suddenly wasn't too appealing. The schools were on lockdown, so no outdoor activities of any kind were allowed. Molly was on the track team, so they were practicing inside the cafeteria. She was running sprints back and forth and slammed into a wall by accident. I had to take her to the ER, as the coach thought she had a concussion. She did. Trying to talk to her was crazy, as she kept circling back to the same question.

"What happened to me?"

"You slammed into a wall at track practice."

"Why was I running inside?"

"Because there is a sniper loose in our area killing people, so we can't go outside."

"*What?*"

"Never mind. Just rest."

Thankfully, they caught the snipers, and that episode was over. The next year we experienced a blizzard in February that shut everything down for weeks, and then hurricane Isabel, the sec-ond-worst storm in history to hit the DC area, paid us a visit in September. It dropped six to twelve inches of rain and left two million people without power. Flooding and devastation were widespread. Trees were down across many of the roads east of I-95. Power was off for almost seven days. Thankfully, my in-laws had a generator that kept their freezer going, so we were able to spare some of our food.

Oh, that all our challenges were so easily solved. Moving to Stafford was a difficult transition for my teenagers. My son, Mike, was forced to leave a huge group of friends in Newport that he had really bonded with. He was the star soccer player his junior year in Rhode Island, but the coaches on his new team in Stafford didn't know him, so he sat the bench most of the year. He was so discouraged, and it truly broke my heart.

He had begged us to be allowed to stay in Newport for his senior year, and several of his friends' parents assured us they'd love to have him live with them. But I just couldn't do it. I don't know if it was selfishness or a wise decision, but we made him come with us. I just felt like we had only one year left with him before he went off to college, and I didn't want to miss his senior year. But watching him struggle with few friends and for the first time not starring in a sport was difficult.

It took Matt a while to find friends also, and when he did, I rejoiced so much that I didn't have wisdom in monitoring what he was up to with them. John made some neighborhood friends quickly, so he was content. And Molly made one close friend, but a year into the friendship, the friend dropped her out of the blue. Not really sure what all happened there, but it devastated Molls.

I feel like all my children reached out for some self-medicating behaviors due to their loneliness and ache to belong. Now, could some of these issues have manifested whether we'd moved them or not? Maybe, but mom guilt is very heavy when her babies are suffering and making some poor decisions. There was drinking going on, some inappropriate relationships, eating issues, sneaking out, skipping school, smoking cigs, and whatnot.

I'd always thought I'd be such a sharp mom since I had been such a rotten teen. I thought I'd be able to spot when my own kids were headed down the wrong road since I'd spent so much time on one myself. Wrong! Or maybe I kind of knew but had no clue how to get them on the right road. Oh, we tried forcing them to go to youth group, made the younger ones go to Sunday school and the older boys help out with children's ministry. We prayed together, ate dinner most every night together, and did all the other activities we thought would keep things on track. We even bought a boat in the hope that they'd love waterskiing and boating and picnicking so much that they'd willingly spend time with us. They loved the first couple of outings, but it lost its appeal fairly quickly.

The one good thing about parenting teens was it truly caused me to spend a lot of time on my knees. I remember my mom telling me she prayed the rosary often on account of my mixed-up soul. She also told me she prayed I'd have kids just like me so I'd know the true hell I put her through. Although I felt I was losing it in the good parenting category, I have to say that I didn't let my insecurities and fears keep me from truly enjoying those years.

Yes, there were some serious problems: The doctor stated he'd hospitalize Molly if she lost any more weight. We couldn't get her to eat normally, and she was dangerously skinny. The father of one of Matt's girlfriends called us at 3:00 in the morning, telling us his daughter was in our basement. Mike came home one night very drunk and sick. John discovered girls and vice versa. I'm guessing you can all use your imaginations here as to why these were problems.

But by the grace of God, they all excelled in school and were launched into the world. And they all ended up liking us with a modicum of respect thrown in. I say that because I recently had a conversation with John (now thirty-two and a major in the army) about those tumultuous days. He said he thought we'd done it just about right. "If you'd been too mean and controlling, we would've rebelled and disliked you. If you'd been too loose and said 'do whatever,' we wouldn't have felt loved. You had a good mix of strictness and trust. You let us make mistakes, and we learned from them."

He might have been trying to make me feel good, as I was apologizing for not being a better mom and keeping him from some choices that ultimately led to hurt. But I include all this here to encourage any of you reading this who are parenting teens. God does send hope when things look overwhelming. He sent me the big picture of parenting, which I took to mean keep the relationship with your kids open, honest, and loving at all costs. You will make mistakes. They will make mistakes. You all will sin, but He is the great Redeemer! You will not be able to control lots of the circumstances swirling around your teens, but God is ultimately in control. He might not do what you ask Him to, as He allows free will to all people at all times—yes, even teenagers—but He's full of grace and mercy and kindness and can be with them when you can't.

I always remembered a time when I was just sixteen and had taken the family station wagon on a drinking spree with my friends loaded in. We drove the country roads drinking and carrying on, and at one point I realized I was headed straight into a concrete pylon. I literally thought we'd all die, but the next thing I knew, we were headed straight down the road again. I honestly think God sent an angel or used His own power to correct the steering and save our lives.

My aunt Maureen was killed in a car crash when she was around that age. Why didn't God save her? I have no idea. It's truly a mystery the way He works sometimes. I realized with my own kids that God has a plan. Obviously, He gives you free will to work out your own plans, and that includes doing dumb things that could bring great harm. But Scripture says in Psalm 139:16, "All the days ordained for me were written in your book before one of them came to be." You go when it's your time to go, and worrying about it can't add a minute to your life. If it's true for me, obviously it's true for my kids. God pulled me to safety when I was being foolish. He will do it for my kids also unless their destiny is different, and my worrying about it will not add one minute to their lives. My prayers in those days went something like this.

You love my kids even more than I do. I find that hard to comprehend when I love them so much it hurts sometimes, yet You loved them so much You gave Your life for them. What lesser things would You withhold? You are for them, always, and not against them, You are with them. I can't get in their souls, but You can. Help them, Jesus! And help this mama do right by them. Amen.

My mom probably prayed similar prayers for me. She used to mutter that she knew God would never give her more than she could handle. Then she'd blatantly say, "I wish God wouldn't trust me so much. He must think I can handle you people and all your problems!"

My own philosophy on this is that God absolutely allows things to come into our lives that we can't handle. Who can handle terrorists blowing up your husband's workplace or violent storms threatening your home or snipers randomly shooting people in your neighborhood? Who can handle teenagers with angst and growing pains perfectly? Not me, and God knew it all along and never had any notion of me going it alone. Jesus graciously sent His Spirit to be an ever-present help in time of need. The mighty Comforter, who never leaves us or forsakes us, was with me in such a beautiful way throughout all the ups and downs, whispering, *Trust Me.*

Our worship pastor at church would remind us all the time, "When you can't understand His hand, trust His heart." I thought it was just a clever cliché until the road I was walking down kept exploding, and it was only through the power of the Spirit reminding me of the God of hope who loved me that I was able to walk it with a measure of joy and peace.

As Mike decided to transition out of the marine corps into the civilian world, I'd need that peace more than ever.

CHAPTER 13

Working for Money but Not Exclusively

*With our first child off to college soon and three more
shortly after, I need to help out financially.
Father, can you help me get a job I'd love—and be
able to talk about You, not just make money?
I guess I'm asking for something meaningful
and enjoyable that also pays.*

Westchester Court, Stafford, Virginia (Still)

I needed a job when we arrived in Stafford, but all I really knew to do professionally was to teach school. It had been years, and I wasn't licensed anymore, but I heard you could substitute teach without a current license, so I went to the orientation meetings for subs and started doing that.

Funny how God leads through different channels. I learned that we could qualify for in-state college tuition in Virginia if I established my own residency apart from Mike. His residency was in Michigan, and we did not pay state taxes there, so he did not want to change his residency to Virginia. But there were so many good colleges in our new state, and we needed to qualify for in-state fees. I needed to make $10,000 in a year's time to be considered a resident, and subbing wasn't cutting it. Plus, it was a very lonely job.

You couldn't really bond with the kids, as you had different classes all the time, and the teachers didn't really want to waste much time chatting with you, as they had their own friends at the lunch table. It felt more like a babysitting job with no benefits than a teaching job. But God used this dissatisfaction and dilemma to help me search for something better.

I learned about homebound teaching, which paid triple what a regular sub made, and you could do it on your own schedule, ten hours a week for middle school and high school, and five hours for elementary. I had the freedom to break it up however I wanted, which was fabulous, but the real joy came in actually having a relationship with the students assigned to me and the freedom to teach as I saw fit. Now, having said that, obviously there was a curriculum we had to cover. But God was so present and real during that job that I was in awe. I had asked Him to give me a job where I could talk about Him, and *boom*, He delivered!

The very first student I had was a high school gal who was on maternity leave. She had just had a baby boy, and I got to work with her for almost a month before she needed to go back to school. I picked up all her books from the high school and got a general syllabus of the work she needed to cover in each subject. As we talked that very first day, I realized she wanted to take raising this precious son of hers very seriously and be a good mama even though she was just sixteen. In my opinion, raising children is hard work, and we need help from the Divine. But I was kind of chicken about bringing up the subject of God because I knew there were all kinds of rules about that, and I didn't want to get fired.

God solved the problem for me by delivering a paragraph in her civics book that literally stated, "Charles Finney believed that in order to improve society in general it would take the personal conversion of each citizen to Jesus Christ."

What? I was so shocked! First of all, that this discussion was in a textbook in this day and age, but second, it was the very first book of hers we looked at and was exactly the spot where she had left off before she had her baby! No one in the world can tell me that was just a coincidence. God was saying, *Tell this precious young woman about me. Don't be afraid!* How could the school find fault with me when I was simply asking her, "Do you understand what this paragraph is saying? Do you know what a personal conversion experience to Jesus Christ even means?"

She had absolutely no idea. I asked her if she would like to know. She said yes. *There you go! An open door, an invitation to speak freely.*

I explained it to her, and then we got to talking about her precious son and how God sends help and hope when we know Him and lean on Him. I'd like to say she embraced it all, but I don't really know. I was educating and explaining, not pushing.

All I know is that, every subject and every day, there was something more. In her literature class we studied the play by Arthur Miller called *The Crucible.* It's a dramatized and partially fictionalized version of the Salem witch trials. It stirred so much real conversation about good and evil, angels and demons, and hypocritical religion versus a compelling relationship with Jesus. Then we studied sections of *Paradise Lost* by John Milton. Oh my, very deep. Truthfully, way over my head, but we legitimately got to talk lots about God because the whole poem is about His eternal providence and seeks to somewhat justify the ways of God to man. I was thrilled to be on such a verbal adventure with God in this young girl's life. Scripture says that "some sow and some reap," and I felt like He'd called me simply to sow the seeds of His goodness into the soil of her heart. He'd take care of the actual reaping.

My next student was a sixth grader who was so clinically depressed he couldn't attend school and was enrolled as a homebound student for the rest of the year. I'm a strong believer in the idea that our bodies, souls, and spirits are completely intertwined, and what affects one area absolutely affects the other parts of us. If we are physically ill, that will affect our mind, will, and emotions. If we are spiritually dead, it will affect our overall well-being of body and soul. If our emotions are allowed to rule our life instead of the mind and will and Spirit, we will suffer all over for it. Third John 2 in the New American Standard Bible says, "Beloved, I pray that in all respects you may prosper and be in good health, just as your soul prospers." Now, I'm not saying you have cancer because your soul is jacked up. I'm just simply stating that what you are doing with your body physically affects your inner being, and what you are thinking about and dwelling on affects you physically. And when you're alive spiritually, you have the power and the desire to align your mind and your will and your emotions to what God desires, and that brings wholeness and a healthiness that is hard to have apart from Him.

Why I mention all this is that my sixth-grade student lived in a very dark trailer filled with cigarette smoke and located on a busy road. He didn't go outside to play, as it was too dangerous. He ate whatever he felt like eating, which was a lot of junk food. He spent a lot of time on violent video games or watching TV with no restrictions and no set bedtime. His grandma was trying to raise him, but she didn't have a lot of energy. She told him she didn't get past third grade, so school wasn't really that important. She was on welfare, his dad was on welfare, and when he grew up, he could just go on welfare, so there was no reason to strive for anything else.

His mom had abandoned him, and he knew it and had a lot of anger and pain as a result. He talked a lot about the other kids his mom had aborted. Why did he even know about that? I fully realized I'd be clinically depressed too if I were him living in this particular physical and mental state! I got him a bike and insisted we meet at the library instead of in his home. I rode over to get him, and together we rode to the library and back every time we met, in the hope of getting him at least a little bit of exercise and some fresh air. Sometimes I took him to a diner and urged a healthy meal on him. I talked to him of the importance of getting enough sleep and keeping your mind away from negative input that feeds the depression.

He said to me one day, "You suffer through school, which I completely hate, just to go on welfare, which you don't even need school for, and then you die. What's the point of it all? I could die now and be out of all this."

I asked permission from his grandma to talk to him about the real point of life, excusing myself from my role as public school teacher, off the clock, just friend-to-friend conversation. She gave her permission, as she knew how deeply depressed her grandson was and had no clue how to help. I shared the gospel with him. I invited him and his grandma to church. I paid for him to go to kids' camp. I prayed for him. Did he embrace it all? Again, I don't really know. He did stop talking about wanting to die, though, so that was some progress. I do believe some good seeds for healthy, fruitful living were planted. I think he caught a whisper of hope from the Divine. I know I did.

God sent me hope that I could have a meaningful, purposeful job and possibly make a difference in someone else's life by leading them to the One who is the Way and the Truth and the Life! The One who actually has the power to change a life. The Mighty Healer who can bring physical, mental, and spiritual health when we cooperate with the wisdom He gives us through various channels. We can't really blame the Lord for not healing our ills if we refuse to eat healthy, get some exercise, limit the trash that goes into our mind, and actually come to Him with humility and belief that knowing Him and obeying Him can make a difference. I knew the Lord could and would heal that precious student of mine if he would cooperate.

One last adventure I'll mention was with a student who lived far back in the woods in a cabin with parents who were hoarders. I'd never seen so much stuff packed into so little space. One subject we needed to cover was an overview of the world's major religions (incredible, huh?). When we discussed Christianity, it was evident she knew nothing of Jesus Christ. When I asked about her experience of Christmas and Easter, it was all about Santa and the bunny. She had watched the Disney Movie *Prince of Egypt*, so she knew a little about Moses. What a delight to get to explain to an eager listener the story of Jesus and why He came to earth.

Now, all this homebound teaching was great and fulfilling, but I still wasn't going to make the needed $10,000. So I got another job. That set me on an incredibly adventurous path. Again, God's sovereign hand was at work bringing help and hope and healing. Help in that I needed another job. Hope in that there were so many new possibilities with this job. And healing in that I found great friends and kindred spirits and a renewed sense of purpose so my own soul was being refreshed daily.

The church we joined in Stafford was amazing. I really have to be moved to cry in public—deeply, profoundly, spiritually moved. The first service I sat in at our new place of worship, I felt the presence of the Holy Spirit and love, joy, and peace emanating from the people we met, and I wept for joy. Mike and I jumped into a big adult Sunday school class, started volunteering and tithing, and became a part of a family quickly. When I realized I still wasn't going to make my $10,000 quota to earn residency, a friend told me about a part-time job opening on the staff at church for a children's ministry assistant.

I applied and held my breath. Could this be such a beautiful answer to prayer on so many levels? Miraculously, I got hired. I say that because I wasn't the most qualified. I knew nothing about computers—zero, zilch, nada. My learning curve was steep. Thankfully, I had good teachers, and God again proved Himself as an ever-present help in time of need. I'd feel overwhelmed and stupid about something I couldn't quite figure out, and I'd take a moment and ask Him for help first. He always sent me to the right person who could take the time to show me how to accomplish the given task.

Months of doing mundane tasks, like recording attendance for each class, typing baptism certificates, and sending birthday cards to kids morphed into the opportunity to help radically transform our ministry to children. The old-school model we'd been operating was one where every age group had a class they were to go to. We purchased a curriculum, then begged people to volunteer to teach it. Very few people really wanted to, and I knew why. It was so boring. Now, there were some gifted teachers who were called to this and made spiritual truths come alive for the kids they met with, but there were many others, like me, who grudgingly gave up one Sunday a month to hand out the assigned worksheets to the fourth graders. This particular age group did not have a teacher "called" to be there, so we roped four couples in to taking one Sunday apiece, or there would be no class. I spent a lot of my time during the week calling people and begging them to take a shift in our nursery and preschool rooms, or we'd have to turn people away.

Thankfully, our pastors knew we could do better than this. We took a team of our most gifted and dedicated volunteers to a church in Chicago that had a premiere kids' program called Promiseland. They were holding a conference to show other churches that your children's ministry could be the best hour of a kid's week. It could actually turn into a place where kids begged their parents to take them instead of having to be dragged there. We all caught fire with the possibilities. They had a curriculum that involved stage sets and props and acting out the Bible stories and singing catchy songs, then crafts that they explained how to prepare and package and were way above and beyond a worksheet. They had games that highlighted the spiritual truth for the week, and meaningful, age-appropriate questions and conversation starters for small group time.

Buying the curriculum was easy, but the hard thing was going to be finding the huge number of volunteers it would take to pull this off. I distinctly remember holding our roster of volunteers up to the Lord and saying, *Only you could multiply this team into the numbers we need. We have thirteen. We need fifty-two. Where will they come from, and how? If You don't help, Jesus, this won't come to fruition! Could you do something like you did with the loaves and fishes?* He did, and it was amazing. Motivated, talented people came out of the woodwork to help with the acting, singing, administrative and greeting roles, small group discussion leading, building stage sets, and decorating the environments to be appealing to kids. We had more than enough volunteers, and none of them had to be cajoled or guilted into helping. They all wanted to be involved in something new and exciting. It was a beautiful thing to behold the transformation of our children's ministry.

God is powerful and wants His Word to go forward. I'd once heard Warren Wiersbe say in a teacher training that it was a sin to bore people with the Word of God. Put some work into your presentations. Put some prayer into your programs. Another cliché that served me well during that time was "Work as if it all depends on you and pray as if it all depends on God. When men work, men work. When men pray, God works."[1]

Boy, did I pray during that season, and God worked. I found out He had equipped me to lead. Although there were moments of fear and trembling at the enormity of what we were trying to do, there were more moments of great joy and enthusiasm as the hard work paid off. Watching kids' faces light up as Bible stories were acted out, hearing sweet, childish voices lifted in worship, hearing sincere questions asked or simple prayers offered up in small group time was so delightful.

God truly helped me get a job that was above and beyond all I could ask or think. I loved it, and I loved learning to trust Him more and more by stepping into the hard situations with specific prayers and watching how He would answer. I made my $10,000 quota, and my son Mike received in-state tuition status to attend the University of Virginia the next fall.

One glaring problem, though, was I was only hired to work part time but was actually putting in full-time hours along with continuing to do homebound teaching. Molly was starting to display some serious signs of an eating disorder and needed my full attention. I was working on a master's degree in Christian counseling with two of my colleagues from the church staff. I could easily handle that in between appointments for her. Thankfully, my son decided to go the ROTC route and didn't need the tuition status for the next year. So I took a break from being a breadwinner.

Another move was in order as Mike left the Corps and started transitioning to a civilian job. We sold our house on Westchester quickly, and for twice what we paid, so we gladly moved to a townhouse for eight months while we had what we thought would be our forever home built in a more rural area of Stafford County. Little did I know that my respite from working would be brief, my struggle with teens would be multiplied greatly, and my cries for help from the Lord would increase exponentially.

Merrill Court, Stafford, Virginia

CHAPTER 14

Seeking Employment Again but Also Empowerment

Mike is a bit concerned about our financial
future and wants me to work full time.
I'm ready and willing, but once more,
Lord, could it possibly be a job
where I could be involved making disciples?
Could You help me get a job again?

What would I do now? I thought I'd burned my bridges at the church, although I was volunteering with women's ministry and having a blast doing that. I was standing at the door to our worship center at church handing out flyers for some women's ministry event we were advertising when our young and fervent student ministry pastor asked me to come work for him. I thought he meant chaperone camp that summer. Lo and behold, he knew the student ministry director who worked for him was getting married and moving on, and he was looking to hire someone.

Once more I felt like I was the least qualified of the twelve people who applied. I really had no experience working with teens, and my own teenagers were certainly not a sterling example of youths on fire for Christ. But newly armed with a master's in Christian counseling, by the grace of God and His will, I got the job.

I love it when in hindsight the leading of the Spirit becomes obvious. I never wanted to be a professional counselor because I thought it would be way too depressing to sit and hear nothing but people's problems all day long. I like to sit and listen and counsel and pray with hurting people, but I also like to be around those who are ready to get out there and do exploits for the Lord. I like to recruit and train and see people employed to do God's beautiful work of leading others into the kingdom and strengthening them to walk strong with Him. So I hadn't been sure why the door to getting a master's in this discipline was so widely opened for me and why I felt compelled to walk through it. Now I knew why. It opened another door to get the job as the student ministry director.

I had only been working with the pastor who hired me for about a month when the church decided to call him to be our head pastor, so all of a sudden I was leading student ministry on my own while the search committee worked to find a new guy. Oh Lord! A couple of the candidates for my job, who obviously hadn't been hired, were part of the volunteer team, and they weren't inclined to help me succeed. I didn't blame them for having sour grapes, but I really needed their help. I literally knew nothing about leading a huge student ministry. The pastor told me he'd help, but that was impossible as he was plunged into all kinds of new responsibilities and couldn't possibly spare the time needed to guide me much.

My prayer life suddenly got energized to whole new levels. I once more learned that real help in desperate times comes from the Lord. I don't often hear what I think is His direct voice to me, but as I poured out my insecure heart to Him, I heard Him whisper, *Just love my people and teach my Word.* I felt a new confidence, and things unrolled. The sour grapes leaders eventually chewed and swallowed and got on board, and we built an incredible team. We went to conferences together and learned so much. My role was more about pouring into the adults who poured into the students, but of course I interacted constantly with the teens also. And it was a joy. I especially loved going to camps and on mission trips and retreats with them. So many really had a heart for the Lord and learning His truths, so teaching and counseling was rewarding. (Sidenote: one of the students that I came to know and love, Kelsey Jo Holt, became my daughter-in-law years later. What a gift!)

In the meantime, life in the townhouse was short lived, a nice chapter in our lives as most of our stuff was in storage, and the townhouse was small and easy to manage while I started my new job. Matt went off to college on a full-ride ROTC scholarship with the marine corps, and son Mike was fully entrenched with an air force scholarship, so things were going well on the home front. But does going well ever last in this life? Not in mine! We moved into our new home, and down the road trouble brewed once more.

Dunbar Drive, Stafford, Virginia

CHAPTER 15

Running from Selfish Ambition

I love my job, but it's
adversely affecting my marriage.
Please send some healing.
And not just of my marriage
but of the bitterness in my own soul
that I have developed from what
I'm guessing might be labeled "selfish ambition."
I can't stand the bitter taste in my mouth
and need healing.

We loved the home we had built out in the country, and working in student ministry the next four years really was glorious. I learned so much, as our head pastor ensured we could go to all kinds of conferences and training seminars so we could continually improve. The problem with student ministry was that I needed to be available when teenagers were free, mainly nights, weekends, and summers.

It was hard, as that was when my family needed me also. Molly would come with me to camps and retreats and such, so I made it work with her, but not so with Mike. His hours at his new job as a watch commander at the Terrorist Screening Center in Washington, DC, were almost opposite of my hours. I rarely saw him. When Molly graduated from high school and headed off to college, my husband requested that I quit my job so we could stop living lives that didn't intersect very much. We didn't need the money anymore. His new job paid well, and the three boys were all on ROTC scholarships (one air force, one marine corps, and one army—talk about service rivalry!). Since Mike had retired from the corps, he had become a Virginia resident himself, so I didn't need to earn in-state residency for Molly's sake.

I'd like to say that I graciously acquiesced to my husband's request, but that would be a lie. I truly loved my job and felt like I could pour even more energy into it now that the kids were all gone. I was starting to get some outside speaking engagements also. I'd been invited to go to England to speak at a women's seminar, then go to Africa as part of a missionary encouragement trip. Now, none of this was paid for except our room and board at the various places. When I asked Mike to fork out the money for plane tickets, he said, "No way! Why would I pay for you to go away again when I have been begging you to stay home more?" It made me furious. In my self-righteousness, I declared that I had supported him all these years while he traveled around the world for the marine corps, so why couldn't he support me now and let me travel all around with church duties?

The cold war raged in our marriage for months. The friend of mine who was coordinating the England and Africa trip kept asking me to confirm that I was going. Finally, I confided in her that I didn't have all the money yet for tickets because my husband didn't want me to go. We had a long heart-to-heart talk, and I confessed what was happening. She was a godly woman and a good friend who had the courage to say a hard word to me. She said something like, "So you're going over to Europe to teach women to love the Lord and obey everything He has commanded, yet in your own heart, you don't want to obey? You know Scripture says we are to submit ourselves to one another in love, and especially husbands and wives."

She made me see that Mike wasn't being demanding or unfair or disrespecting my right to work and travel but simply wanted our marriage to be a healthy one. I was so convicted because as she spoke I knew she was dead right. I immediately called Mike and told him I didn't want to go to England and Africa anymore if it was going to cause so much contention between us and that I would quit my job tomorrow because I cared more about him and having an intimate marriage than I cared about traveling and working. I told him that I suddenly realized he truly did have my highest good in mind.

I was completely taken aback with his response. He said that this declaration of mine meant more to him than our wedding vows. He also said he didn't want me to quit my job tomorrow but just wanted me to be open to discussing it. And then he said he wanted me to go to England and Africa. Not only would he pay for the tickets but would lavish me with some spending money also. What a glorious lesson to me—that God does want to help us when we are frustrated with something or someone. He does want to heal our marriages when they are fractured, but we have to cooperate. We need to know His Word, and we need to want His will more than our own.

I worked in student ministry another nine months but made it clear I'd be resigning at the end of that school year. At one point a job opening for the pastor of adult ministries became available. I desperately wanted to apply but was told, "We have real pastors applying, so don't waste your time."

I knew I had as much education as the rest of the pastors on the staff. I had years of experience in different ministries. I knew and loved many of the people I'd be working with. Why wasn't I qualified? Obviously I wasn't an ordained pastor in the denomination, but couldn't they just change the title to minister or director and let me lead?

To be fair here, I knew in the Baptist world women were considered helpers, not leaders. I learned all about "Complementarianism," a theological view that men and women have different but complementary roles and responsibilities. Women are held to be equal in moral value and of equal status but can't function in certain roles and ministries within the church body. So headship roles go to men and support roles to women. I understood this on some level, as I was raised Catholic, where women couldn't be priests, only nuns, which in itself was cool, but they always had to be subservient to the priests. I held more to the egalitarianism view that roles should be ability based and not gender based. This obviously is a controversial subject, and my conclusion of it all is that there are many godly people in different denominations that adhere to both sides. Kind of like the tongues controversy, I knew where Tommy stood on this issue, and I also knew where my friend Sam stood. I decided it was something I could agree to disagree on and move forward with the clear direction to, "go and make disciples," however that might play out.

So I couldn't lead, but I could be the assistant to the man they hired to be the pastor. Truthfully, at the time I was excited to have that role. Once more I got to be part of the thrilling adventure of seeing God transform a ministry. Adult ministry was operating similar to our old children's ministry style. We had classes by age groups on Sunday mornings. We did have quite a fabulous women's ministry going on that was thriving in both outreach and "in-reach," but our Sunday morning attendance in groups was at best a couple hundred people, and our church had almost three thousand people on the rolls.

We sought to change that by starting home groups. Once more, we needed tons of new leaders if we were going to provide groups. *Where would they come from, Lord?* I won't bore you with the details, but through much prayer and the grace and power of the Holy Spirit in response, we went from twelve Sunday-morning classes to eighty-two small groups meeting in homes. We had almost one thousand people involved in some kind of smaller setting where they could talk about the Bible, the sermons they'd heard, and how it applied to their actual lives. People were connecting and finding hope in real relationships, help in their trials, and even healing in their spirits as God became more tangible to them and His great truths more understandable and applicable.

The beginning months of this new job were so exciting, yet all these crazy things started happening in my family. My oldest son called and said his fiancée, Vanessa, had cancer and was losing her health insurance, so they needed to get married quickly in our back yard. My second son called and told us he was leaving shortly for Afghanistan and would be in the thick of the fighting over there. My third son called and was involved in an accident, and the father of the girl driving the other car was taking him to court and suing him. My daughter called with debilitating health issues and wanted to drop out of college. The IRS called to let us know we were being audited. Our veterinarian called and said the tests on our dog showed cancer throughout, and we needed to put him down.

I sat in my overstuffed blue chair where I met with the Lord each morning and laid each problem at His feet. All of a sudden it hit me that, just possibly, all this happening at once could be kind of a spiritual attack to distract and dishearten me since we were trying to do something at work that might help a lot of people. I defiantly declared out loud, "Satan, if this is you, I'm not afraid of you. Greater is He who is in me then he who is in this world. Jesus has triumphed over you already, and I belong to Him, so you will not bring me down."

Then, very stupidly, I added this: "You think you can scare me off? Well, bring it on!"

Now, some of you might scoff at this, but I'm telling you the truth of what happened next, although I know it's bizarre. I went upstairs to get ready for work. As I took the first step to descend our long staircase, I tripped somehow and fell all the way down. I jumped up and wasn't hurt. It felt a bit miraculous that I hadn't broken anything. I got in the car, and on my way to work, a huge rock smashed into my windshield. The impact was so loud and hard, I jerked the wheel and almost crashed but got the car righted in time. The rock didn't leave any mark at all on the glass. Next, I drove around the corner, and there was a whole flock of turkey vultures right there in the road, and they flew up and surrounded the front of my car. At that point, although I was a bit freaked out, I turned on praise music and started singing at the top of my lungs, and eventually peace and confidence flooded me once more. But I have to admit, I learned not to taunt the evil one. That just isn't smart. Resist him, as Scripture says, and he will flee from you, but daring him to bring it on won't go well.

So my son Mike got married, my son Matt survived the war in Afghanistan, my son John won the case against him, and my daughter, Molly got on some good meds and returned successfully to school. The IRS audit showed we were honest, and our dog— well, he did die, but he was old. And things at work just got better and better.

After starting all those home groups, we realized that one size does not fit all when it comes to groups that can help people grow. We started realizing that many people had serious issues that had created spiritual roadblocks for them, and they needed help moving those boulders off their path so they could move forward. So we started what we called care groups. We offered marriage courses, parenting of prodigals, Celebrate Recovery (addressing all kinds of addictions), divorce care, PTSD groups, GriefShare, and more. We added core groups that helped introduce people to faith and create a sturdy foundation of basic doctrines so they would be well grounded before they joined a home group.

I thought it was all miraculous and marvelous and the mighty hand of God at work through us. But as often happens, there were different philosophies on how to do things. We had all read an innovative book called *Simple Church: Returning to God's Process for Making Disciples*.[1] Basically, it said to quit offering all kinds of options for people. Just ask them to come to church on Sundays, serve somewhere, and be in a home group during the week. It was an interesting proposal for how to make disciples in this day and age. One staff member said to me, "I really wish we could blow up everything you've started here. It's too much. It's too complicated. We needed to just offer home groups and keep things simple. But now you've messed that up, and I don't know how we can fix it." I really understood his mindset because of the things we were reading on how thriving churches were now doing things differently.

If you are wondering why it was all blamed on me and not the adult ministry pastor I worked for, it's because he gave me lots of freedom. Then he quit, which left me fully in charge to do what I wanted. Was I fooling myself? Was this whole movement not of God but simply me being bossy and pushy and liking to start new things?

That was the beginning of a season of discontentment. Something ugly started growing in my soul. I felt resentment and a growing bitterness that I knew was not pleasing to God, but I couldn't seem to change. *Why do I have all this responsibility for adult ministry and none of the perks that the "real pastor" had before he left? Am I not doing the job of an adult ministry pastor? Why then, am I making a third of the salary he made? Why is my office a converted closet decorated and paid for out of my own salary versus the nice office with good furniture? Why don't I get a seat in the meetings that matter?* (Side note: I recently saw *Hamilton* on Broadway and completely empathized with Aaron Burr as he sang about wanting to be in the room where it happens.)

I kept wondering if this was what James in his epistle called selfish ambition. *Why do I care so much? Do I crave status? Do I need the appearance of success in this church world?* Things progressed to the point where I needed to be free from the internal angst of it all. I wished I were more humble and could honestly say my motivations were pure. I wasn't and I couldn't. I cried out for inner healing.

What came was the prompting to step away totally from this job. I wanted to blame everything on being a woman in a man's world, but I had to face the humbling fact that I just wasn't the girl for the job anymore. I prayed and prayed for clarification because I loved my job, despite the resentment. I loved the people I worked with. How could I leave my "family"? It was a painful decision and one I wavered in until the Lord gave me a verse that shored up my confidence in knowing it was the right decision. "You will go out in joy and be led forth in peace" (Isaiah 52:11).

Now some of you readers might be thinking, Well, that was obviously in the Old Testament talking to the Israelites. Why would you take it personally? Because the Father talks to His children personally through His Word. If you expect to be spoken to personally when you read the Bible and not just generally, then when you sit down and talk to God and ask Him for direction, for wisdom, He gives it to you freely. Often He does this through a verse that jumps off the page, metaphorically speaking, and resonates loudly in your soul, and you have a sudden knowledge that He has spoken—not just to the Israelites in a story, but to you in the twenty-first century.

I was teaching a course at the time called Alpha, and one of my favorite lessons to teach was "How Does God Guide Us." I was so convicted by my own voice teaching . . . sounds ridiculous, but it's true. Everything I was telling others about God's guidance applied to me right then and there about my own decision-making. The Alpha lesson uses alliteration to help us remember the ways God guides today when you can't really hear Him with your physical ears or see Him with your eyeballs. He guides us through:

- Commanding Scripture: He won't counsel you to go against His Word, so check that first.
- Compelling Spirit: He's in you both to will and to work for His good pleasure. Listen to the Spirit within you as you pray.
- Counsel of the Saints: Get opinions from others who are filled with the Spirit.
- Common Sense: He's given you a mind. Use it well.
- Circumstantial Signs: Is there a door opening or closing? Test it.[2]

I knew God was telling me to close out the chapter in my life story that was all about working church ministry so He could start writing a new chapter. I did go out with joy and peace. Little did I know at the time how much fun and adventure was ahead for me, or I would've added some dancing and singing to the peace I was feeling. Part of that adventure was another move!

Turnstone Court, Stafford, Virginia

CHAPTER 16

Wanting His Will More than Mine (Kind Of!)

Lord, I'm putting my hope in your Word
that says You've prepared good works
in advance for me to walk in.
I know You lead your people;
I just need hope that I'll clearly hear you
and not miss out on any of those good works.
And we are moving again, Lord!

We spotted a house being built in the neighborhood behind ours and watched the progress being made as we'd take our evening stroll. As it neared completion, both Mike and I fell in love with it. The property was charming, the house designed with so much light and beauty. Even the story of its builder was intriguing. He was from Uganda, and he'd design and build one big house on this tract of farmland he had bought, and then sell it and take the profits back to his home country to invest in good works there. Then he'd come back and build another one.

We decided if the Lord would sell our Dunbar House quickly—this was just before Thanksgiving, and we said we'd only keep the house on the market till Christmas—and have the builder of the new house come down a bit in price so we'd almost break even, then it would be a good use of our time and money. We closed on Christmas Eve and moved into our new house in January.

The beauty of it all was we had so much space to host a myriad of different gatherings. We had so many dinner parties and hosted sleepovers of all kinds. One of my favorites involved a dear friend of mine, Susan Wanderer. Susan and her husband Ed adopted three children from Ethiopia, and in the process, she made friends with a myriad of other women adopting children from the same country. One of those friends happened to be the author of a Bible study I was leading at the time. We decided to hire her to do a conference at our church and then host any of the other moms in this "Ethiopia group" as our guests. Twelve of them came, and they all stayed at my house. Oh, the stories that were shared that night!

So home life was fun and I was enjoying my new freedom from a structured work life.

The way ahead of me for ministry did seem like it was going to be an adventure. I did eventually find a pool of joy, but in retrospect I realized I kept rushing the pace of the journey and never took the time to slow down and get honest about my hurt feelings and confusion along the way. I wanted so desperately to have a positive spirit about this big life change that, when things didn't go well, I shrugged it off and moved on. Not necessarily the healthiest way to cope in this world, especially when you know the Healer of hurts personally. Why not be honest with Him about the pain? He knows anyway. I struggled for a couple of years trying to find my niche.

Because I'd worked on the church staff for fifteen years, I assumed once I resigned, I'd still be known and valued. I actually thought the church would benefit because I would still work hard but wouldn't get paid anymore. Such a deal! What I hadn't counted on was the fact that I was no longer part of the strategy-making team, so when I had ideas as a volunteer, they were rejected because they didn't fit the vision.

After being on staff, I understood the behind-the-scenes stuff, and I fully realize you can't do everything people want you to. I also know that God has put authorities over you, and the willingness to submit to authority shows humility that God wants us each to embrace. Let's just say this was a hard season for me because I didn't know how to turn off the part of me that loved to create new pathways for people to connect and engage with God, so I kept trying to get the church to do things my way. It seemed the church had pivoted without me, and I was left feeling lost.

Again in retrospect, God was moving me on from traditional church ministry to something brand new. I know that His sovereign hand moves in mysterious ways and that sometimes hurtful things happen for a reason, and we don't have to be bitter about it but recognize the good that can come from it all. But I also think we do ourselves a disservice if we don't deal honestly with our woundedness. Maybe writing it down here is cathartic and a small way in which God brings healing. Bring junk into the light, and suddenly the darkness in the soul disappears. It all seems rather petty now and prideful on my part. A prayer I'd picked up from some admired author writing about true humility was "God, give me an un-offendable heart."

I thought I'd learned some humility, but I'm guessing that character trait is never fully developed until we see Him face-to-face. God doesn't seem to yank a prideful heart out of a person but helps a person make the choice to not be offended. I read that gratitude is "an internal air freshener" (this from one of our podcast guests, Dr. Alicia Britt Chole) and that choosing gratitude is a spiritual discipline that makes us more like Him. It's natural to be grateful when everything goes our way and works out the way we think it should. It's supernatural to choose to be grateful on a regular basis as a discipline of life. And it makes the soul sweet and "sploshy" with prints of the Holy Spirit oozing out (again Dr. Chole's imagery. If we could be like sponges fully saturated with the Holy Spirit, then everywhere we went, He would splosh out of us and leave His marks).[1] I chose to be grateful that God was directing me even in my somewhat wounded state. The pool of joy in ministry awaited me, and it all started with the friend I just mentioned, Susan Wanderer.

Susan was the family minister at our church and my buddy while I was on staff. We went to all kinds of conferences together and really enjoyed each other's company even though there was a twenty-year age difference between us. I literally could be her mom, but with her bubbly, warm, accepting personality, she never made me feel anything less than a peer. We had done a couple speaking events together and seemed to complement one another in our different styles. Once I left the staff, we didn't cross paths for a couple of years. Until one Sunday, we ran into each other after a service. She invited me to go to a conference with her. It sounded like an adventure and a good opportunity to catch up with Susan, so off we went to Nashville, Tennessee.

Turned out the conference was about podcasting. Susan declared on the trip down that she thought we should pair up and do a podcast together. "Susan, I'm not even sure what a podcast is! I mean I've heard sermons preached on what I guess is called a podcast, but I don't really know what you mean about joining you to do one ourselves."

I was about to find out exactly what she meant. The conference was hosted by Annie F. Downs, and basically, it was her doing a live podcast recording in front of all the attendees. She interviewed various guests and added her commentary. I remember leaning over and telling Susan, "This is just like an old-fashioned radio show . . . an announcer or hostess interviewing people. I get it! But I don't think I'd be the best partner. I'm old and I'm not really funny. I also can't think fast on my feet and be spontaneous with deep spiritual truths. I'm more of a scripted speaker, more of a teacher using a lesson plan."

She urged me to just stay open to the idea. As the weekend progressed, we met all kinds of other women who were either already podcasting or considering starting one. We gathered lots of good information, along with just having a blast together shopping and eating and talking and worshiping. On the long drive home, we brainstormed together what this new endeavor might entail. I realized that I wouldn't have to be a comedian or a spontaneous wisdom spouter, as we would simply interview women with interesting stories. They could be the funny or wise ones. Between the two of us, we came up with a list of almost one hundred women who we knew had very interesting stories. It was truly a compelling idea, but I was still a bit unsure if this was what God had in mind for me. As we pulled back into Stafford, Susan asked me to please pray about it and let her know in a couple of weeks if I was in or not.

I did pray. I also listed all the reasons why I should not say yes to this, one of them being I'd already said yes to a lot of other opportunities. I was serving on two boards, a mission organization, and a church network association. At that time, I was still involved in military ministry in our area, and we were doing all kinds of events. I was teaching several Bible studies over on the marine corps base at Quantico. Overcommitment seemed to be my MO. It really didn't make sense to add another thing. The whole idea kind of scared me. When I thought about having to talk spontaneously to an audience, I'd break out in a sweat. It led to nightmares.

After one particularly exhausting night, I settled into the cozy nook where I met with the Lord each morning and poured my heart out to Him. I asked Him to please give me some direction and make it clear. It was ironic that I was once more teaching the lesson in Alpha on "How Does God Guide Us?"

So, in applying this teaching to my own plea for guidance, I started with Scripture. I had just taken a Bible study on the book of 2 Timothy taught by Beth Moore. The theme of the book seemed to be that each of us is entrusted with the gospel and then equipped and encouraged and empowered to share it with others. Acts 14:1 says the apostle Paul, along with his friend Barnabas, spoke the gospel so effectively in the Jewish synagogue in the city of Iconium that a great number of Jews and Greeks believed. In the opening session of this Bible study, Beth implored us to note this verse and then ask God to blatantly ramp up our own effectiveness at sharing the gospel. I had prayed that prayer often throughout the summer months as we studied this beautiful pastoral letter.

It was now September, and I'd been given an open door to a ministry where I might be able to actually do what I'd been praying about. God vividly brought all this to my mind as I asked Him to guide me in this decision.

But I felt like I needed to remind Him of all the reasons this wasn't a good fit for me. After pouring out my list to Him again, I said, *Forgive me for doing all the talking and not listening well. Open my ears to hear you.*

I picked up the version of the Bible I was reading at the time, *The Story* by Max Lucado. I just started reading where I'd left off the day before. I was in awe! Only God could take a story written thousands of years ago, about a guy named Moses, and use it to answer my modern-day plea for direction. I read about God calling Moses to a task and Moses explaining to God why he couldn't do it. God's response back to Moses felt like a personal response to me and my excuses. As best as I can recall, this is how Moses and I talked to God and what He said back:

Moses: Who am I that I should go to Pharaoh and bring the Israelites out of Egypt?

Me: Who am I to do a podcast with Susan? She'd be better off with someone younger, more hip.

God: I will be with you.

Me interpreting God: *Doesn't really matter who you are, Katie. If I call you to do something, I will be with you, and that's qualification enough.*

Moses: Pardon your servant, Lord. I have never been eloquent. I am slow of speech and tongue.

Me: Lord, I'm not spontaneous. I can't think fast on my feet. I need notes and practice and such, or I'm a blathering fool.

God: Who gave human beings their mouths? Who makes them deaf or mute? Who gives them sight or makes them blind? Is it not I, the Lord? Now go; I will help you speak and will teach you what to say.

Me interpreting God: *Duh! Doesn't really need interpreting! Pretty direct!*

Moses: Pardon your servant, Lord! Please send someone else.

Me: Oh Father, I think this is a great idea, but maybe I could just recruit someone else to be Susan's partner, and I could help in some other way besides speaking. Maybe I could help produce the podcast somehow?

God (gets angry at Moses for his refusal to trust and obey): What about your brother, Aaron the Levite? I know he can speak well. He is already on his

way to meet you, and he will be glad to see you. I will
help both of you speak and will teach you what to do.

Me interpreting God: *Katie, you know Susan, your
sister, can speak well.* [We had done some speaking
engagements together in the past, and she was always
a big hit with audiences.] *She will be glad to partner
with you, as she's all ready to do so. Quit worrying, as I
will help you both speak, and I will show you what to
do.*[2]

So the Spirit of God used the Word of God, along with an
open-door invitation to a new ministry and counsel from my husband and a few friends, to guide me in making a decision that,
from my vantage point now as I write this, almost three years later,
was one of the best decisions I could have made. I went from ignorance of the podcast world to actively engaging in it.

Susan and I bought two microphones. She got her teenage son
to show her how to record on GarageBand and bought something
called an RSS feed. We set up on my kitchen table, and the first
couple of episodes were us telling our own stories.

Then we had our first guest, Donna Tyson, a much-sought-after international speaker. The military ministry I was still working
in had hired her to do an event, so I asked her if she'd mind being
on our podcast while she was in town. Susan and I knew nothing
about Zoom at this time, so we were limited to guests who could
sit at my kitchen table.

Donna knocked it out of the park, telling her story of making
it big in corporate speaking circles, enjoying the money and the
fame, but then being called to sell everything, give up her lucrative
speaking career, and go to Haiti. Her brother was there helping
those who'd become destitute due to the devastating earthquake in
2010. She found peace and freedom living simply and ministering

daily as needed. Best of all, she found an intimacy with the Lord she'd never known before.

Then she was diagnosed with an aggressive breast cancer and forced to move back to the States for treatment. She had no home, as she'd sold everything when she moved to Haiti. She had no health insurance. Things were bleak. Explaining how the Lord took care of her through those scary circumstances, Donna's face shone with palpable joy. At the end of the interview, she said she wouldn't trade her cancer journey for anything. She sounded like Job in the Bible, who after losing everything, including his health, says something like, "I'd heard of the Lord, but now I've seen Him." She oozed intimacy with our Savior. I wasn't skeptical really of what she'd said because I trusted her sincerity, but I wondered how Jesus could make such a frightening time sweet. Little did I know that I'd find out the hard way in a couple years' time.

After Donna, the guests started rolling in! Even though we were limited in our skills, God sent us some amazing women with stories that always featured God as the hero. We had Sharon Glasgow, a popular speaker with Proverbs 31 Ministry for women, telling a miraculous story about building their broken-down barn into a beautiful wedding venue on practically a zero-dollar budget![3] Michele Husfelt, the wife of an air force chaplain who was serving in the White House, told her story about moving to a high-rise apartment building in downtown DC to be part of a neighboring ministry.[4] Rebecca Lyons, a best-selling author and speaker, told her story of living in New York City and loving the hustle and bustle and diversity but being sidelined by debilitating anxiety.[5] They each had big followings and influence, so that helped our little mom-and-pop (although there was no pop, so mom-and-mom) podcast grow. We were so excited.

Again, hindsight is twenty-twenty. Why wasn't I promoted on the church staff? Why didn't my volunteering work out like I thought it should? God had a better plan for me. Part of that plan involved letting me experience disappointment, even bitterness. He didn't want me to be the kind of person who just skimmed over real emotions that trials in this world bring. He wanted to show me that faith isn't living in denial of the hard things; it's bringing the hard things to Him and letting Him transform us by the renewing of our minds. In other words, letting Him give a perspective on relationships and circumstances.

Jesus Himself said to the Father, "Not my will be done, but Thine." Jesus had perspective on all that happened to Him on earth . . . the good and the bad. He entrusted Himself to the One who judges righteously. I needed to do likewise. Going forward, I started echoing Jesus—somewhat. My prayer was *I want to want your will more than my own.* Selfish ambition is ridiculous, and I don't want any of that in my heart or mind. Doing the podcast with like-minded women was exactly what God had in mind for me.

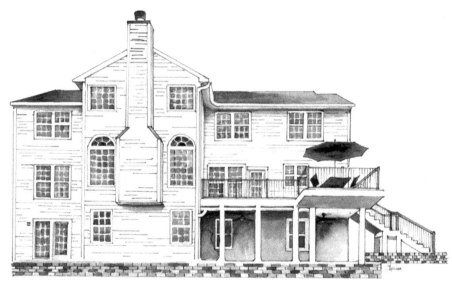

Wateredge Lane, Stafford, Virginia

CHAPTER 17:

Relying Heavily on God's Provision

We don't know
what we are doing.
Will you send help
with both the podcast
and another move?

I n wanting the will of God for my life increasingly more than my own, I started thinking we should downsize. The home we'd purchased was perfect for a season, but I felt like it should be turned over to a big family to enjoy. We needed to find a smaller one. I mentioned to my type-A husband these thoughts, and by the next week we had looked at a model home in a fifty-five and older community, loved it, selected a lot to build on, and put our big house on the market.

It sold almost immediately. Once more our new one wouldn't be built in time to do a door-to-door move. Thankfully one of my best friends had a two-bedroom basement apartment built for her son and his family, but they had recently moved out. She graciously rented it to us for the next nine months. Don't think basement like in dark and dreary: think walkout with lots of windows overlooking a backyard pool, professionally landscaped, but also backing to thick woods. It was gorgeous and restful, as we had very little housekeeping responsibilities, leaving plenty of time to focus on the podcast.

Things with the podcast were going well, but we quickly realized the microphones we had purchased were subpar. We needed new ones, which cost $150 each. We also needed to figure out how to record guests who weren't local. Our monthly costs were adding up. We knew we needed a website and some kind of social media strategy, but neither of us was adept at these kinds of things, and hiring someone would cost money we didn't have. I'd never been part of a ministry that had no backing from a church or chapel. I'd always had access to some kind of budget, along with team members with varied skills who could help move the ministry forward. Now it was just Susan and me with whatever personal money we could scrape together and throw into the pot. We were a great team on air, but we had a lot of the same strengths and weaknesses.

As we grew in listeners, we knew we needed to improve on what we were producing. But it was going to take money and gifted people to help. We really had no clue how to raise the money or where to find people who would want to come on board. We spent a lot of time asking God for help. For the first time in a long time, both of us were completely dependent on God moving to make things happen. We stood in amazement at how He provided step-by-step.

I was chatting with a young military wife, Olivia, at a luncheon and talking about the podcast ministry and our challenges. I was truly just making conversation, but she said, "Did you know that I'm a financial consultant, and I have helped nonprofits get started? I'd love to help you get organized."

She put together a whole financial folder for us and urged us to become a 501c(3) nonprofit. We needed a lawyer, though, to represent us. Susan's father-in-law, Dean, who just happens to be a lawyer, volunteered his time on our behalf. Shortly after we were granted our nonprofit status, I came into a little inheritance money and was able to use it to help fund some things. Then my beautiful children started chipping in. They all started giving donations in one form or another. Susan and her generous husband, Ed, continued to pay most of the monthly bills. We had enough money each month to do what we felt called to do at this point.

The next beautiful movement was when God started sending willing volunteers to help us on a long-term basis. I met with an old friend, Gwen Curtis, who had recently retired from a church staff position and had been praying for God to show her where to pour her energies next. She knew about the podcast, but neither of us connected her plea to God with our needs until she said, "What I loved the most about my job on the church staff was helping people tell their stories. I loved being able to coach people to bring their thoughts and words together in a concise and compelling way. Then watching them share their story and seeing the impact they made on others was so rewarding."

It hit me. "Hey, you love stories! Our podcast is all about stories. Would you consider helping us somehow?"

All of a sudden we had a story curator, and things went to a new level. Instead of Susan and me telling guests, "Well, just tell your story. *Go!*" we actually started having a process where Gwen would contact the guest and do some preparation prior to our recording day. She honed stories down to highlight different aspects of what might be shared and then scripted questions for Susan and me to ask while we recorded the episode. She researched each guest a bit on social media and gathered some facts in order to create an interesting bio we could use to introduce our guests. You can imagine how this improved the podcast.

Right after Gwen joined the team, we decided to take a road trip. Susan's friend and long-time mentor, Susan Blount, lived in

Minneapolis and invited us all to come visit. Susan B. had been coaching Susan W. for years in both her ministry endeavors and in life. She was a big fan of the podcast and was willing to spend some time investing in us with some sage advice and a trio of interesting guests for us to interview. We decided to drive and stop along the way and interview fun people. Gwen had a best friend in Ohio with an amazing story, and then we stopped in Wisconsin and interviewed a bunch of my family members. My brother Mike owns his own lobbying-marketing business in Madison, my brother Tom pastors a large church there, and my brother Jim is a marketing director for AARP. The wisdom and direction these precious family members and friends poured into us during this trip was priceless. We learned so much and used time in the car on the way home to brainstorm and strategize future plans.

One of the real pearls we collected on that trip was a new team member. Portia Allen was one of the guests Susan B. had lined up for us to interview, and when she and her husband, Clinton, walked into the loft in downtown Minneapolis where we were staying, there was an instant bond between us all. It's hard to put into words, but as we were introduced and started chatting, there was a familiar feeling in the air like we were already deep friends. We found out later that Clinton was a songwriter-worship leader and had actually authored some of the worship songs we'd been singing back in our home church in Virginia. How cool is that?

Weeks after the trip, Susan made a statement that changed our little "mom-and-mom" podcast to something so much bigger and better. She said, "We need to ask Portia if she will cohost with us."

My immediate thought was the Scripture in Ecclesiastes 4:12 (NLT) that says, "A person standing alone can be attacked and defeated, but two can stand back to back and conquer. Three are even better, for a triple braided cord is not easily broken."

This piece of wisdom proved so true in the coming years of the podcast. Little did Susan and I realize there would be many times one of us wouldn't be available for various reasons to interview all the important guests God was sending our way. When God added Portia to our team, not only did she bring stability to our weekly recordings, she widened our circle of influence and brought a new depth and richness to the commentary we add while interviewing.

We had a few more very generous donations and were able to hire a friend named Colin Mukri to create a website for us. Things were coming together slowly but surely—such a beautiful unfolding of the reality that when God calls us to do something and we pray and trust Him, He will, in His time, provide the help needed. We now had some cash, some new helpers, and some forward movement. And the guests coming our way were incredible.

We figured out how to record long distance, and one of the first from far away, from Uganda actually, was Katie Davis Majors. She wrote a book called *Kisses from Katie*, which had been on the *New York Times* Best Seller list. At eighteen, Katie moved to Uganda and eventually became the adoptive mother to thirteen girls. She just passionately wanted to make a difference in this world, and after visiting Uganda on a missions trip, she knew her calling was to return and care for orphans there. Oh my, the challenges and heartaches and sacrifices she faced, yet the joys she experienced were all incredible.

Irene Rollins, a pastor in Baltimore, was another stunning interview. Alcoholism crept up on her as she enjoyed a glass of wine each night, then two glasses a night, then more. Then enjoying the wine turned into needing it. But as a pastor, she couldn't see herself as an alcoholic, so she fought her husband when he suggested she might have a problem. After all, she was pouring her whole life out helping others; how could she be messed up? Her story of being set free by intervention from family and friends, incredible counseling from professionals, and the overwhelming love and power of her Lord and Savior is one to listen to.

Anna LeBaron's story had me sitting on the edge of my seat. She was the daughter of the infamous polygamist cult leader Ervil LeBaron. She had more than fifty siblings! Her story involved incredible poverty, horrific living conditions, sexual grooming, child labor, and more. She eventually escaped the cult and gave her life to Christ and started down a path of healing and recovery. She wrote a book called *The Polygamist's Daughter*, which was a page turner.

Women like Margi McCombs, Kim Hyland, Sharie King, Jessica Honegger . . . sharing trauma and heartbreak and loss and restoration in beautiful and honest storytelling moved me to tears week after week. And there were many others. At some point I'd love to write a book that just featured the stories we've gathered over these past years.

Susan was able to get feedback through one of the platforms we were on and see how many listeners we had and where they were listening from. We were amazed when we hit over one thousand listeners on every continent except Antarctica. We had a small pocket of people listening in from Iran! Oh, that we could possibly be encouraging some women with hope in dire circumstances!

Never in my wildest dreams did I imagine myself filling out government forms to start a nonprofit, cohosting a podcast, chatting with a huge variety of talented amazing women every single week, helping to organize live events that were beautiful and impactful, and loving it all. I'd always held on to the truth found in Philippians 2:13: "For it is God who works in you to will and to act in order to fulfill His good purpose" and had found I was living that out in many of the different seasons of my life, but never had I felt it so strongly. I felt like Eric Liddle in *Chariots of Fire* when he said, "God made me fast. When I run, I feel His pleasure." God's pleasure in what we were doing was so obvious to me and filled me with joy and the willingness to keep going.

He made Susan and Portia and me chatty. He made Gwen creative, with the ability to help craft stories. When we came together and showcased stories that could help change listeners' perspectives on God and faith and how to thrive despite trials, we felt His pleasure. Relying heavily on Him in times of doubt and confusion and need is a sure route to inner peace and lots of outward joy. We couldn't help but smile lots in those glory days. I never would have dreamed of the nightmare days that would follow.

Burbank Ave, Fredericksburg, Virginia

CHAPTER 18

Living Loved

I don't fear dying from this aggressive cancer
that's been diagnosed, but I'm scared
I won't be able to handle chemotherapy and that
I'll embarrass myself and You by my weakness.
I fear I'll discredit my faith in You.
Can you fill me with hope?
I need biblical hope. Hope that You've got this.
Hope that when I am weak, You are strong.

When it rains, it pours. The year 2019 brought so much action I could hardly keep up. It started well with some beautiful trips, one to Israel in January and one to California in February. The trips were tied together in a way, as I was going to be speaking to a group of women in Twentynine Palms, California, which I've already mentioned is in the heart of the Mojave Desert. I would be teaching about a psalm that was written in the desert lands of Israel, a message I'm sure the ladies there would be able to relate to.

The women's ministry coordinator at Palm Desert Baptist Church, April Erhardt, and I had talked extensively about the theme in Scripture for that year's conference. We settled on Psalm 42:1–11 (NIV), which some Bible scholars think may have been written by King David while he was running from his son Absalom, who was trying to kill him. Others think it was penned by the sons of Korah but written for King David and his inner angst.

> As the deer pants for streams of water so my soul pants for you, my God. My soul thirsts for God, for the living God. . . . Why, my soul, are you downcast? Why so disturbed within me? Put your hope in God, for I will yet praise him, my Savior and my God. My soul is downcast within me; therefore I will remember you from the land of the Jordan, the heights of Herman—from Mount Mizar. Deep calls to deep in the roar of your waterfalls; all your waves and breakers have swept over me. By day the Lord directs his love, at night his song is with me. A prayer to the God of my life. I say to God my rock, "Why have you forgotten me? Why must I go about mourning, oppressed by the enemy?" My bones suffer mortal agony as my foes taunt me, saying to me all day long, "Where is your God?" Why, my soul, are you downcast? Why so disturbed within me? Put your hope in God, for I will yet praise him, my Savior and my God.

I remember sitting near a waterfall at the headwaters of the Jordan, gazing upon Mount Hermon in the distance and pondering what King David might have been feeling. I made a short video for the women in Twentynine Palms—from one desert to another. "Are you downcast? Are people around you wondering where your God is because of what is happening in your life right now? Can we learn from King David how to preach to our own souls? Can we put our hope in God?" I had no idea as I was crafting that message that it would primarily be for me this upcoming year. I did, however, have a sense that some big shift was coming.

We spent the last days of our trip to Israel in Jerusalem. Our tour guide gave us a little talk before he let us spend an hour on our own in the garden of Gethsemane. He said, "Keep in mind that Jesus Christ did not want to go to the cross. But because He loved His Father and wanted to do His will, not His own, he went where He didn't want to go and did what He did not want to do."

He said if we were true Christ followers, we would want to do the same. As I leaned against an old, gnarled olive tree in the garden and poured out my heart to God, I knew I was heard, and something would come of it. I admitted to God, *I really don't want to go where I don't want to go, and I really don't want to do what I don't want to do.* But I was willing for Him to make me willing, whatever that took. I asked Him to strip away everything in me that was superficial and holding me back from being more like His Son, Jesus.

The stripping started that March in what felt like a whirlwind of activity. We had previously sold our big home and had a small one built. So as move-in day approached, there were all kinds of house things to be done: new rugs and furniture to order, carpenters hired to deal with bookcases that needed to be added, landscapers and patio builders to be met with, not to mention paperwork and banks. At the same time, my father-in-law was admitted to the hospital with cancer.

I tried to visit him daily, as we were the family who lived closest to him. His wife, my mother-in-law, had died the year before, and he missed her terribly. After the first chemotherapy treatment, he decided he'd rather just go home to heaven and be with his dear Evie and not pursue any more treatment. We met with social workers, and their opinion was that he was not clinically depressed and was in his sound mind and therefore should be allowed to make that decision. He pretty much stopped eating and drinking and died shortly after we moved into our new home. We planned the funeral and had to go through all his things and close down his apartment.

In the meantime, I'd discovered a lump in my breast. I really didn't think too much about it because of cysts I had in the past that only needed to be aspirated. I was convinced that this was just one more of those. But of course, I couldn't ignore it, as cancer runs so rampant in my family. So I dutifully went first to my primary care doctor, who ordered a mammogram, then the mammogram appointment, then a sonogram appointment, and then the biopsy.

I was so busy with not only the new house, the funeral, and closing down Dad's apartment, but also all kinds of ministry events, that I didn't really have time to worry as we waited to hear the results. I was teaching several classes over on the Quantico Marine Base and planning closing ceremonies for those. Our podcast was having a huge live event at a local barn, so there were lots of meetings and shopping to be done for that. My son Matt, his wife, and three of my grandchildren were moving to California in June, so I only had a couple months left to spend with them and wanted to make the most of it. I was trying to plan dinners and outings and such with them. And I had signed up to go to a church conference in Atlanta with the staff and elders of our church.

Although I wasn't worried about the lump in my breast, my husband was. He really didn't want me to go to the conference, as the timing was the same week the results from the biopsy should be delivered. But the tickets were all paid for and everything arranged, and I really was excited to go. So off I went with the heartfelt promise to stay alert to my phone at all times and call home as soon as I heard something.

The conference was in Atlanta at a church called Northpoint. It was so inspiring and informative that I just lost myself in the teaching and worship and fellowship. Somehow my phone didn't get charged in the hotel room like I thought it would have, and of course, I missed the call from the doctor. When I tried to call back, my phone died. A nice Northpoint person led me to a charger, but for some reason I was so rattled I couldn't even plug it in. Thankfully, two of my closest friends surrounded me and said they would wait with me until I could get hold of the surgeon.

I jumped a mile when my phone finally rang. The last session of the conference had started, and everyone was inside the worship center. I walked down one of the long halls attempting to go outside to be able to focus better on what the doctor was telling me. It all felt so surreal when he said I had a very aggressive type of cancer, triple negative breast cancer, stage 3, and would need to come in immediately for consults to start treatments. Telling my husband, Mike, and then my daughter, Molly, was so emotional. I told them to spread the word to the rest of the family, and I'd talk to them all that evening.

As I slipped back into the conference, the crowd was singing one last worship song together, the same one we'd been singing all week. I decided it would be my theme song for this season. The song, "Bigger than I Thought,"[1] is by Sean Curran of Passion and speaks of bringing all our fears and failures to Him and stopping any kind of negotiations. For some reason the lyrics just seemed to fit the situation perfectly.

The conference wrapped up, and our group loaded into our vans and headed to a nice Mexican restaurant for a final dinner together. My spot in the van was between Brian, one of our associate pastors, and Mark, one of our elders, and I talked nonstop the hour and a half to the restaurant. I was filled with adrenaline and needed to release it. Those poor guys got an earful of my philosophy about the Lord's healing powers.

I told them about my first experience with a loved one having cancer. My mother had breast cancer when I was very young in my faith. I had absolutely no expectation of God healing her. The cancer spread from one breast to the next to her lymph nodes. She had a radical mastectomy and more surgery in the lymph nodes. The chemo treatments made her wretchedly ill. She admittedly thought she was on death's door. But then came a miracle. My brother Tommy came into her room one night and told her he felt like God had told him to lay hands on her and pray for her to be healed.

She looked at him, took a drag of her cigarette, and on the exhale said, "Oh, what the hell! It can't hurt."

Tommy prayed over her, and by her own admission, a presence entered the room, and she knew she was healed. Now, she said you can call it what you like, but she knew that something shifted inside of her. My mother was fifty-two when she was diagnosed with cancer, and she lived to the ripe old age of eighty-seven. The cancer never came back. After that, I fully believed God could heal anyone at any time in any way!

Now, I had to tell the pastor and the elder all about my dad and my sister dying of cancer but being fully restored spiritually and how, as sad as the physical death was, the spiritual life was real and vibrant. I went on and on and on . . . telling them that I felt like the apostle Paul and I had a lot in common when he wrote to the Philippians from a Roman jail. He said something like "For me to live is Christ and to die is gain! I'd much rather leave this world and go be with the Lord but I think it's better for your sake [speaking to the Philippians], that I stay on" (Philippians 1:21).

I surmised that I really wasn't afraid to die of this cancer, but I felt too young and had a lot of work left to do in the world, and perhaps it would be better, especially for my husband and beloved daughter, if I lived on. My sons were all married and starting families, so I figured they'd be fine without me, albeit sad. But I sure would like to get to know my grandbabies. And our podcast had just started bearing fruit. So much to live for, really. Would He choose to heal me like He did Mom and leave me here on earth, or take me home to heaven like He did Sheila and Dad? Well, either way, I knew I was in for an adventure.

Brian and Mark just kindly listened and let me rattle on. What I experienced the next couple days and months was the body of Christ at its finest. Immediately, all the friends I was with gathered around me at the restaurant and said kind, comforting, caring things. They prayed over me and truly made me feel loved and valued.

Texts started pouring in from family. The words from my marine son, Matt, were so profound and beautiful that they became sort of a mantra in the coming days, just like the lyrics of that worship song. Matt said (my paraphrase of his text), "The verses I was reading in my quiet time this morning were from 1 Thessalonians 5:16–18. 'Rejoice always, pray continually, give thanks in all circumstances; for this is God's will for you in Christ Jesus.' When I got the news of your diagnosis, Mom, the application of what I had read that morning came to me very clearly. We all need to adopt the right attitude and pray for God's strength, encouragement, and understanding. This is a very applicable model for all of us for how to deal with this cancer season."

That night, phone calls came from my sons and daughters-in-law, my brothers and sisters and in-laws. There were more precious conversations and prayers. Susan and I were rooming together, so she was a witness to all the drama unfolding. As we finally turned the light off to try to get some sleep that night, I told her very honestly, "I'm really not asking, 'Why me?' I'm saying, 'Why *not* me?' You and I have been interviewing women with hard stories. But in one way or another, God always rescues them. And it's been fascinating for us to hear the stories. Now maybe it's just time that we live a tough story ourselves."

We decided that night that we would record a podcast episode the next day and share about the diagnosis and that this season of walking through cancer would be one of our ongoing stories highlighting how God sends hope, help, and healing into an ordinary person's life.

The next eighteen months were definitely a tribute to the ways in which God works when we ask for help. Specifically, He sent an expert, caring medical team. He flooded me with gifts and words of encouragement from many of His children and others. He had books delivered to me that contained wisdom and gave meaning to much of what I'd endure. He showed me so much about myself and the important things in life that I'd never have learned without the suffering. He deepened the relationships I had with family and friends in a way I didn't even realize I needed or dream was possible. Bottom line, my cancer journey was an answer to prayer in a weird way. I'd prayed for three distinct things over the year leading up to this fateful one:

- I prayed that God would deepen my understanding of what it means that He is "with" us.
- I prayed to never have to experience a "dark night of the soul" unless it would truly deepen my relationship with Him and not ruin me.
- I prayed to have all the shallow, surface stuff in me stripped away and that I'd actually desire His will instead of my own.

Let me unpack a bit what prompted each of these prayers so you understand how going through a bit of hell on earth was a needed trip for me.

What prompted this first prayer was a book I'd read that deeply affected my faith journey, *With: Reimagining the Way You Relate to God,* by Skye Jethani.[2] Basically, Skye uses four prepositions to outline the ways many of us think about relating to God that are so wrong. We often misconstrue that life is led *under* God, *over* God, *for* God, or *from* God. They are all based on the idea that we need to control God to alleviate our fears and bring about the kind of life we want here on earth. Skye asserts, and I agree, that all religions are truly based on this idea of somehow controlling the supernatural forces around us in order to ensure safety in this hard world.

Life *under* God is the idea of trying to cajole, manipulate, and appease a higher being with my actions so he will protect me. Think of ancients with their sun god and rain god and such and the rituals they'd come up with to ensure a successful harvest or hunt. Christians? *Well, if I pray right, fast, read my Bible enough, then God owes me protection—right?* My religious rituals and behaviors pull the strings to get God to do what I want.

Life *over* God is the idea that I don't really need God Himself in my life. Obviously atheists live this way, but Christians? Often we embrace God's principles and decide that is the way to control life. If I raise my children "God's way," then they will be good and I won't fear. If I handle my finances "God's way," then I'll be rich, so I won't have financial worries. Certain pastors don't see much need for prayer because they know basic business principles that work and will run their churches that way quite successfully. So I am the one pulling the strings by employing the principles that will ensure my safety, and God Himself need not be a part of it.

Life *from* God is basically the notion of God being a genie or a vending machine. The way I relate to Him from this position is that, because He loves me, He needs to give me what I want when I want it. So I call the shots, and God's role is to provide.

Life *for* God is the idea that if I work hard for Him, then He owes me protection. The harder I work or the more self-sacrificing I am (think missionaries in African jungles or pastors who give up any kind of normal family life to be at the beck and call of their congregations), then the more God owes me in return. My mission becomes the important thing, and God obviously needs to line up with that and cooperate.

They are different approaches, but all are attempts at control, and every one of them falls short. In some cases, they actually increase our fears because our attempts at control are never enough! So rather than producing peace and tranquility in our souls, many forms of religion function like a treadmill with the speed being gradually increased. We run faster and faster to gain more and more control, but we never arrive at our destination.

I could clearly understand the four ideas of relating to God that were wrong. I also clearly saw how I'd subtly believed each one in different ways over the years. I repented. I confessed. I changed my theology! But I only kind of understood the real way we need to relate, the final preposition Skye used. God wants to be "with us."

In the author's words (emphasis mine):

> In the gospel of John it says, "In the beginning was the Word and the Word was with God and the Word was God. He was in the beginning with God." Jesus being the Word came in the flesh and dwelt among us. Immanuel, *God with us.* The posture of life with God is predicated on the view that *relationship* is at the core of the cosmos, *not self, not laws, not mission, not some capricious will, but a real intimate genuine relationship with God.*[3]

I understood that, from the beginning, God created men and women to live in relationship with Him. It got marred by sin, but Jesus went to the cross to fulfill God's desire to be with us. His death took away that sin, that barrier, and then when we surrender all to Him, we lay down that pride and selfishness that says, *My will be done*, and we desire His will. We desire to walk His ways, we give up control, we desire unity with God—to be with Him, not to control or use Him. I understood all that to a certain extent. I just wanted the understanding to be such an integral part of me that I would naturally relate to God like this and never slip into the controlling position again; hence, my prayer.

Praying about avoiding the "dark night of the soul," if at all possible, was prompted by a sermon I heard by John Mark Comer of Portland, Oregon. He described his own journey into a dark time of depression and how desperate he was to emerge out of it. A mentor told him clearly to embrace the season, as there would be a lot to learn and gather that would come no other way. He hated that answer, but after some years of struggling yet pressing on day by day, the season passed, and he was the richer for it. *Ugh!* My soul shrank from hearing that such an amazing, Spirit-filled teacher could experience such heaviness of mind, such bleakness in the emotions, such lack of experiential intimacy with Jesus. Because if John Mark could go through that kind of hell on earth, then no one might be spared, especially the likes of me.

I've already explained the third prayer's origin to you. Standing in the garden of Gethsemane and honestly asking God to strip away anything shallow and pretentious in me and make me willing to do His will instead of my own maybe should have reminded me at the time of my first two prayers. Truth be told, I only put it all together when I faced the surgeon who would be in charge of my case. He said, "This is a life-changing diagnosis. You have a very serious, aggressive type of cancer, so we are going to use everything we have to combat it. It will be very hard on you. You will be one very sick woman. I suggest you set aside your day timer." I had it out to show him all the dates I couldn't possibly be available for treatments due to speaking engagements, trips, family responsibilities, and so forth.

I was so naïve as to what I was actually facing. "Cancel everything," he instructed, "for at least the next nine months."

Everything? Nine months? Yikes!

I prayed, *God, I know I wanted to know deep down what being with You really looks like and that I conceded my tendency to want to tell you what to do instead of simply saying, "Thy will be done." I have a feeling, though, that a very dark night of the soul is going to come upon me. I don't like to be sick, and it's not just a normal dislike that all sane humans have; it's a complete and utter fear of being sick, nauseated, and unable to cope. So although I prayed those things and meant them, can I change my mind? Can You just miraculously heal me instead? I'd prefer that. I'll tell everyone! And You will be glorified.*

His answer: *No. I am with you. My grace is sufficient for you.*

I knew I was in for an adventure with some scary turns. He gently reminded me of a favorite analogy I'd stumbled across in my early days of walking with Him. And it helped somewhat.

A Tandem Bike Ride with God

I used to think of God as my observer, my judge, keeping track of the things I did wrong, so as to know whether I merited heaven or hell when I die. He was out there, sort of like a president. I recognized his picture when I saw it, but I didn't really know him.

But later on, when I met Jesus, it seemed as though life was rather like a bike, but it was a tandem bike, and I noticed that Jesus was in the back helping me pedal. I didn't know just when it was he suggested we change, but life has not been the same since I took the back seat to Jesus, my Lord. He makes life exciting. When I had control, I thought I knew the way. It was rather boring, but predictable. It was the shortest distance between two points.

But when he took the lead, he knew delightful long cuts, up mountains, and through rocky places and at breakthrough speeds; it was all I could do to hang on! Even though it often looked like madness, he said, "Pedal!" I was worried and anxious and asked, "Where are you taking me?" He laughed and didn't answer, and I started to learn to trust. I forgot my boring life and entered into adventure. And when I'd say, "I'm scared," he'd lean back and touch my hand.

He took me to people with gifts that I needed, gifts of healing, acceptance, and joy. They gave me their gifts to take on my journey, our journey, my Lord's and mine. And we were off again. He said, "Give the gifts away; they're extra baggage, too much weight." So I did, to the people we met, and I found in giving I received, and still our burden was light.

I did not trust him at first, in control of my life. I thought he'd wreck it, but he knows bike secrets, knows how to make it bend to take sharp corners, jump to clear high rocks, fly to shorten scary passages. And I am learning to shut up and pedal in the strangest places, and I'm beginning to enjoy the view and the cool breeze on my face with my delightful Constant Companion, Jesus.

And when I'm sure I just can't do anymore, he just smiles and says, "Pedal."[4]

So Jesus took me first to people with gifts of healing. Doc Strawn and Doc Lindenburg, my surgeon and my oncologist at Fort Belvoir Hospital, were off-the-charts smart, capable, and caring.

They ran every test in the book on me to be sure the cancer had not spread. The brain MRI was the worst. I thought it would be no big deal, as the other MRIs hadn't been a problem. But when the tech told me I had to lie perfectly still and then slid me into the tube, I got a terrible pain in my right arm and shoulder. I had been given a buzzer I was supposed to push if I needed help. I wondered if I was having a heart attack and if I should push the buzzer. I wondered if people died in MRI machines. I wondered if maybe they'd pull me out dead. The anxiety started to ramp up, and of course, that made the pain worse.

I whispered for help—from God, not the MRI tech. I chuckle now as I think of the ways God helped me. One thought that was crystal clear was my mother's voice saying, *Oh Kathleen, you're so dramatic! I've never heard of anyone dying in an MRI machine, and you certainly are not going to be the first! Stop making a mountain out of a molehill.* Shortly after that, this song we'd been singing in church flooded through my mind: "I'm No Longer a Slave to Fear."[5] I calmed down mentally, which somewhat lessened the physical pain, and the test was finally over.

After all the testing, Doc Strawn called and asked if I wanted the good news first or the bad news. The good news was I did not have cancer in my brain or lungs and probably not in any of my lymph nodes either. The bad news was my appendix was diseased and needed to come out. He said the breast cancer needed to be addressed first with chemo and surgery, and then we could take care of the appendix.

After six months of chemotherapy and a lumpectomy, Doc Strawn removed my appendix. My follow-up appointment with him was funny. He said, "No one is ever grateful for breast cancer. But you should be. Your appendix was filled with cancer. Appendix cancer is rare and very hard to diagnose. So you probably would have remained asymptomatic until it burst. And once that happens, no treatment is possible, and you die. But because of your breast cancer, we found it in time. I was able to remove it all."

Back to the bike analogy, it seemed like we had just taken a sharp curve and then flew over the rocky places and landed safely on the other side of the path.

It wasn't just people with gifts of healing He brought to me; He brought people bearing gifts of all kinds. People came out of the woodwork to bless me. I was deeply touched but actually a bit embarrassed. I wanted to say, *Don't use your valuable resources of time and money on me. You have better things to do with them. I'll be fine. I'll be self-sufficient.*

Until God showed me clearly that this was prideful. I had asked for His help to get through this season. He was trying to send me help through His people, but I was being so prideful that I was refusing the help. It was kind of ludicrous actually. Reminded me of that old joke:

> A fellow was stuck on his rooftop in a flood. He was praying to God for help. Soon a man in a rowboat came by and the fellow shouted to the man on the roof, "Jump in, I can save you." The stranded fellow shouted back, "No, it's okay, I'm praying to God and he is going to save me." So the rowboat went on. Then a motorboat came by. The fellow in the motorboat shouted, "Jump in, I can save you." To this, the stranded man said, "No thanks, I'm praying to God and he is going to save me. I have faith." So the motorboat went on. Then a helicopter came by and the pilot shouted, "Grab this rope and I will lift you to safety." To this, the stranded man again replied, "No thanks, I'm praying to God and he is going to save me. I have faith." So the helicopter reluctantly flew away. Soon the water rose above the rooftop and the man drowned. He went to heaven. He finally got his chance to discuss this whole situation with God, at which point he exclaimed, "I

had faith in you but you didn't save me, you let me drown. I don't understand why!" To this God replied, "I sent you a rowboat and a motorboat and a helicopter! What more did you expect?"[6]

My brother Tommy told me simply, "Kate, we've got to live loved to live love."

The message that resonated in my soul was simply "You need to learn how to receive." And learn I did! What a blessing!

The people who surrounded me astounded me. I had a very terrible, twisted idea of love that I didn't even know I held. It wasn't a conscious, reasoned-out idea, but the helplessness I found myself dealing with revealed it. Deep in the core of who I was, I believed people loved me because of what I could do for them. My husband loved me because I ran the house, cared for the kids and our social life, listened to his dreams and plans, and fulfilled his sexual needs. My kids loved me because I was there for them growing up, helping meet their needs, and now that they were grown, I was there to listen and love and pray. When they all came home, I made it as fun as possible with great meals, comfortable beds, waiting on them, and doing whatever activities they enjoyed. My church family loved me because I worked countless hours to further the mission there. My extended family and friends loved me when I showed up for reunions or gatherings and added to the fun. Once I lost all my energy, all my ability to do for others, I felt completely worthless. *Why would anyone want anything to do with me?*

My precious daughter, Molly, challenged this notion immediately by declaring she was coming home for a month to take care of me. I, of course, worried about her job being jeopardized, but she said she had the ability to work from home, and if her bosses wouldn't grant it, she'd quit. Her dad, of course, said, "No way. Stay put and work."

But Molly was tenacious and declared she didn't care what anyone said . . . she was coming to be with me. She went to all kinds of appointments with me, including the first chemo treatments and the first attempt to buy a wig. Receiving her unconditional love gave me courage and lightness as I faced the unknown. Those first hours hooked up to an IV in a little cubicle in the oncology ward of Fort Belvoir Hospital proved to actually be quite entertaining because of her company. She made me laugh so hard I was crying. Silly stuff really, like scooting around on the doc's chair that had wheels and getting yelled at by a nurse and having the chair taken away from her. Why is that funny? I don't know, but we howled.

I had previously met with my oncologist, and we had discussed every detail of my current state of health to ascertain how aggressive he could be with the chemo. He stated that he thought I was in great shape apart from cancer, so he was going to give me the works. I'd neglected to tell him the most embarrassing secret I'd held for years about my health. I had contracted herpes in my younger, promiscuous days, and I was deeply ashamed of that fact. I felt it made me dirty and would disgust people if they knew. Whenever I was overstressed about something in life, I'd have an outbreak. Needless to say, my first day of chemo, the sores were huge and painful. I couldn't ignore it; I felt I had to tell the doctor because what if the chemo mixed with the herpes virus and did horrible things to me?

So again, this is not a funny situation at all, but when Doc Lindenburg popped in to check on me prior to the infusion starting, I bared my soul to him, and he really didn't know what to say. I didn't just state it as a medical fact. I stumbled around explaining that I used to be a crazy person, but I'm not like that anymore and haven't been for years, but sometimes we have severe consequences for behaviors even though we are forgiven for them. It was like he was a priest in the confessional instead of my oncologist just trying to give me some chemo. He was a bit startled.

After some thought, he said it wouldn't matter. But then he looked at me suspiciously and asked if there was anything else I hadn't told him.

When he left, Molly and I laughed so hard—not at him, just at the ludicrous situation and how insane it was for me to go on and on. But I also think I could laugh because her love was so genuine for me and sincere that, in front of her, I didn't have to be something I wasn't. I didn't have to perform. I didn't have to have all the answers or even know the right questions. I could look like an idiot in front of her because she simply loved me for me.

My brothers and sister insisted on coming. Mike assured them it wasn't necessary to spend all that money (plane tickets from Wisconsin and California, time off work, rental car, and so forth), as he and Molly could handle everything. They said they didn't mind and just wanted to be with me. I warned them that I would be no fun. Nothing would put them off. What a gift of love! What a true picture of God being a real help in time of need, as I believe they were prompted by Him to come no matter what.

The five days they were with me were some of the hardest on me physically, as I'd contracted bronchitis and could barely breathe. Coupled with the horrible side effects of the chemotherapy, I literally thought I would die. I had to be admitted to the hospital, as the ER doc and my oncologist wanted to keep an eye on things.

For some reason I slept like a baby that night in the hospital. Mike stayed with me and was my beautiful champion all night long, but he had to get to work the next day, so Tom and Jim and Denise arrived at the hospital early that morning with a deck of cards, and we promptly started playing bridge right there in my bed. We perused the room service menu and strategized how we would have lunch delivered to us all. We were making so much noise and having so much fun together that each nurse and aide and tech person who popped their head in wondered what I was even doing there. They must have conferred with the discharge doctor, because before we could even enjoy our lunch, they decided to release me. We laughed so hard at the speed at which they got rid of us. The adage that laughter is good medicine is so true. I felt so much better.

Throughout the next year and a half of treatments, they all came numerous times, sacrificing so much just to be with me. Receiving that kind of love was an ointment to my soul.

My husband very blatantly addressed my skewed understanding of my self-worth. I was standing in our bathroom looking in the mirror shortly after losing all my hair, letting the tears pour down. He came around the corner and saw me before I could hide my sorrow. He asked me what I was thinking, and I blurted out the truth. "I'm hideous. I am so ugly. Even if you could ignore that, we can't have sex. I can't cook or clean. I'm impatient and unfocused and no fun at all. How can you love me?"

Mike was actually shocked. He took hold of my trembling chin and made me look in his eyes. He tenderly asked, "Is that how little you think of my love for you? That it's based on selfishness? What you can do for me? Have I somehow given you that impression over the years? If so, forgive me. I love you because you're you. I love you more deeply right now than I ever have."

Throughout my treatments, Mike's actions spoke louder than his words. He'd kneel by my bed at night and hold my hand and pray over me. He'd bring me toast and coffee or soup and crackers on demand. He took copious notes on the various treatments, kept track of appointments and medicines, and gave me shots when I needed them. He brought me books and mail and jigsaw puzzles and anything else that might entertain me. He set up a Caring-Bridge site on the internet and kept all our loved ones informed of what was happening. And then he'd read me people's comments.

He took such delight in each response, and reading them together was a little spot of joy and warmth amid a cold, dark time.

Most of all, he encouraged me day after day with his faith that I was doing well and would beat this thing with God's help. I feared that I wasn't working hard enough to beat it. I feared that I was pampering myself and being a big baby and that other people with cancer still worked full time and took care of small kids, and I refused to get off the couch. *If I die, it's my own fault.* Why all the self-doubt and self-hatred? I don't know, but it was another dark strain inside of me that God decided to shine the light on.

If you don't love yourself appropriately, how can you love others well?

People kept saying how strong I was. I kept thinking, *Why do they say that?* I said, *Lord, I'm not pretending to be strong. You know how weak I am!*

He said, *When you are weak, I am strong! Therefore boast all the more in your weaknesses.* That's where my hope throughout all this cancer season came from. To steal the title of a favorite book, *Hope Has a Name.* It's Jesus.

Walking into the oncology ward one morning for another dose of the "red devil" chemo they were giving me, I had a moment of pure panic. I said, *Lord, I can't do this. I can't willingly submit my veins to this poisonous onslaught, because I know the terrible things it will do to me.*

He said, *I am with you.*

And like Mike's declaration of love, it wasn't just words. My love language is quality time, so God sending His people to be with me at various times was such a powerful way for His presence to be manifested to me through them.

My boys and their wives all made it a point to take leave and spend time with me. My Molly came from NYC repeatedly, sometimes for a week or two at a time. I couldn't cook for them, arrange beds or outings, even offer good conversation, yet they gave up vacationing elsewhere to be with me. Many a night we all piled into my big bed and shared stories and songs and jokes and sometimes prayers. One Sunday morning, we all watched the church service together on my computer from my bed—seven of us lined up, squeezed in tight, praising God and listening to His Word.

The gals in my prayer group would come over almost every Tuesday morning. It really helped to simply have something so positive to get out of bed for. My oncologist warned me that spending too much time in bed would be very detrimental, but it was the only place I really wanted to be. I'd have to get up to let my friends in, and then I'd stay up because they all were so patient with me. They'd let me drone on, not making sense or repeating what I'd already told them. Brain fog is a real thing when you are on chemo. Other times they'd let me just sit and stare into space while they chatted around me, making me feel part of things happening even though I wasn't really. Each week they'd bring soup or beauty supplies or vitamins or a new head scarf, and sometimes they'd clean up the kitchen or look around for some other chore to do.

Susan and Gwen came weekly to record the podcast with me, and they weren't averse to having to crawl into bed with me and broadcast from there. One of the dark thoughts I struggled with at the start of this season was the idea that God was shelving me. I felt like I'd messed up somewhere, hadn't been good enough, pure enough, so He'd had to just take me out of the game. The reassurance of Gwen and Susan coming weekly and validating that I could still have a place at the ministry table, no matter how garbled my thoughts and stumbling my speech, was so important to me. It was like thumbing our nose at Satan and showing him clearly he wasn't getting a victory here in calling me off task even if I'd be temporarily limited in how I could "go and make disciples."

But what was more of a blessing than me getting to give out my words to others was the community that poured into me each week. Again He showed Himself strong when I was so weak by teaching me to receive. He made it clear that if I wouldn't receive the love of our podcast community and rejoice in it, then in essence I was shunning His love. I felt like our podcast existed to showcase other women's stories of great faith and I was just a facilitator to make that happen, so being the focus made me uncomfortable. I wanted to hide, not in shame, really, but just because I didn't want to be seeking my own glory, if that makes sense. God showed me that was scrambled logic. There's a difference between seeking glory for yourself instead of for God and being able to give God glory by receiving the love and gifts and kindness that His people lavish on you. I knew that I'd truly never let all the kind words go to my head and think too highly of myself (my mother's voice again: *Kathleen, never believe your own press*), but I would recognize that each act of love poured on me would be a cause to celebrate the goodness of God in others.

In essence, I felt God say to me, *I called my people to love one another. If everyone were always on the giving end, who would receive? Don't pray to me for help and healing and hope if you are going to spurn the people that I've sent to be my hands and feet.*

It's one thing to occasionally receive good gifts. It's another to have a whole season on the receiving end with nothing to give back. God taught me so much about unconditional love by lavishing me with it from others. He taught me to be kinder to myself so I could be kinder to others. Never have I lived so loved, and my great hope is that going forward, I'll be more equipped to love others well.

But it wasn't just the presence of people and their actions that God used to help me thrive, it was words—so many words!

CHAPTER 19

Chewing on
Wise Words

Burbank Avenue, Fredericksburg, Virginia (Still . . . for Life?)

The words of some of our guests on the podcast were truly heaven-sent to me as I walked through this valley. Some very directly, like Ashleigh Burnette,[1] Jane Marczewski,[2] and Dr. Alicia Britt Chole,[3] who spoke eloquently of their own cancer journeys. To be able to share with someone who has been where you are in your pain and fear is such a gift. While we were interviewing these beautiful women, I lost the sense of recording a podcast and truly felt like I was having an intimate conversation with someone God had sent my way for such a time as this.

Ashleigh had the very same kind of cancer as me, developed the same sores, neuropathy, runny nose, and all the indignities of hair loss and wigs and weakness. But she lived and thrived and was better for it all. Jane was given a death sentence by her doctors, causing her husband to walk away from their marriage, as he couldn't handle it. Yet she was healed, both body and soul, and has a beautiful ministry now. (Since I wrote this sentence, Jane's cancer is back, but she has been granted a worldwide stage for such a time as this through winning the golden buzzer on *America's Got Talent*. Jane's a singer and composer that goes by the name Nightbirde. Google her and watch her incredible performance of an original song she wrote called "It's Okay.") Dr. Alicia shared so much wisdom that I can't even begin to unpack it here, but I know the Lord led me to her for continued healing in the future, healing of my soul, as she has a mentoring ministry I aim to be part of someday.

Other guests helped me with their attitude and perspective. So many, but one who stands out right now is Tiffany Johnson,[4] a young mother of three who had her arm bitten off by a shark while snorkeling on a vacation in the Bahamas. Her story of hope and help unequivocally sent by her Lord and Savior sent chills up my spine and made me want to have the same kind of resilience.

And then there was the great help I received from various authors. I know it might seem odd to feel really close to people you've never met and probably never will, but I was strengthened and moved in deeply profound ways by so many different books I read. As I cast around for hope and help and healing, it came in by the droves through the written word of many who I believe were equipped by God to send out wisdom.

The first book I was prompted to read was *Disappointment with God: Three Questions No One Asks Out Loud*[5] by Philip Yancey. I didn't want to read this. I picked it up to give to Molly to read. I wasn't asking those three questions:

> "Is God unfair?" *God, I know You aren't unfair. Life isn't fair, period. But You are perfect, so if You think I should have this cancer, then it's okay.*

> "Is God silent?" *God, I know You aren't silent. I can't hear You very well, but it's my lack, not Yours.*

"Is God hidden?" *God, I know You aren't hidden. You've made yourself known through creation, through Jesus, through the Bible, through the inner witness of the Holy Spirit. I can't see You right now, but I'm sure You're there.*

You see, I had the right answers! I'd learned in an early Bible study that if you are experiencing a disappointment in your life, you change the D to H and add a space after the S—and you get "His appointment." I was all set to do that. Shaken, not stirred, like James Bond's martinis . . . maybe shaken by this cancer, but so calm and cool and collected in my faith that I wasn't all stirred up. I was going to glorify God, be nothing but light in this darkness. I would protect His reputation in front of people accusing Him of not taking good care of me. I didn't need to read a book about being disappointed with God! That book was for Molly.

She wouldn't take it. It sat on my nightstand and beckoned me. And then the reality of chemo drugs surging through my system caused a great inner darkness; my light flickered and faded, and I couldn't see anymore. I kept trying to change the D to H but wondered why this cancer had to be His appointment for me.

Read the book, Kate! It's one thing to have all the answers in your mind and another thing to have them way down in your heart.

This book was such an honest look at the disparity between our concept of God and the realities of life. If He loves us so much and is all powerful, why does He let us seemingly be ruined by disease? If He loves us so much and wants a relationship with us, why doesn't He speak up louder, more directly, when our hearing is impaired?

Yancey talks about Joseph in the Bible and all the horrible things God allowed to happen to him: sold into slavery by his jealous brothers, falsely accused by his boss's wife, and consequently thrown into jail and left there for seven years. Yet Scripture says repeatedly, "God was *with* Joseph." There's that premise I'd been trying to fully embrace. God's presence is the blessing, the miracle, the answer . . . not getting our circumstances to line up the way we want them to. Whether we feel Him with us or not doesn't negate the reality that He simply is. The author says:

> We may experience times of unusual closeness, when every prayer is answered in an obvious way and God seems intimate and caring. And we may also experience "fog times," when God stays silent, when nothing works according to formula and all the Bible promises seem glaringly false. Fidelity involves learning to trust that, out beyond the perimeter of fog, God still reigns and has not abandoned us no matter how it may appear.[6]

Maybe God deliberately pulls back sometimes and lets people or rogue cancer cells harm us to allow our faith to mature. Joseph eventually says to his brothers, "What you meant for evil, God meant for good" (Genesis 50:20).

Yancey talks about all the miracles God did in sight of the Israelites—the parting of the Red Sea, bringing forth water from a rock, His cloud by day and pillar of fire by night over the tabernacle, manna appearing on the ground six days a week to feed His people—and how those miracles never really secured the people's love and affection for Him. They constantly grumbled against Him. They wanted their will, not His, so miracles obviously didn't impress them much for the long term. That made me think of wanting to want His will. My will was a miracle healing quickly so I wouldn't have to go through something hard. His will was for a more intimate walk with me, to increase my trust in Him, and to work this walk through the valley of the shadow of death for my good.

Philip Yancey mentions the idea of a three-part pattern—tragedy, darkness, triumph—seen over and over in Bible stories, especially poignant in Good Friday, Holy Saturday, and Easter Sunday: our Lord's tragic death; the darkness in the hearts of His followers as they grieved and feared and waited, not really knowing that He would rise; and then the triumph of the resurrection. Yancey says, "This is a template that can be applied to all our times of testing."[7]

The shock of the cancer diagnosis seemed tragic. There was going to be a long period of darkness (and here we have the "dark night of the soul" experience that I'd hoped to never have), of not knowing whether I'd make it or not, but there would be triumph! One way or another, I would triumph over this cancer.

After addressing a lot of underlying insecurities in my faith with this book, I started reading stories of people going through harsh trials and actually living out their faith at the same time. I was drawn to stories of disaster.

A friend sent me Laura Story's book *When God Doesn't Fix It: Lessons You Never Wanted to Learn, Truths You Can't Live Without.* She is a Christian songwriter and worship leader, and one of her songs, "Blessings,"[8] had been playing in my head on and off. The lyrics are basically questioning the nature of trials. Have you heard the saying, "It was a blessing in disguise"? This song kind of epitomizes that thought but with questions, not statements.

I loved that song, and the words took on new meaning now that I was facing the hardest trial of my life. But reading her book and knowing what prompted her to pen those lyrics on the back of an envelope while she was sitting in a parked car gave me a whole new level of appreciation for the questions and thoughts proposed. Her husband of one year, the love of her life, developed a serious brain cancer, and surgery did not restore him totally. He lived through it but lost all short-term memory. He could no longer work or be left alone for long. Laura became the breadwinner and his caretaker when her plan had been to have babies and be a stay-at-home mom. As I lay awake night after night with the chemo burning in me, sometimes I'd hum parts of Laura's song about sleepless nights helping me know Jesus more intimately.

I heard that Anne Graham Lotz had been through breast cancer, so I read her latest book, *Jesus in Me: Experiencing the Holy Spirit as a Constant Companion*. Sorrow upon sorrow for her: The church she and her husband had been a part of for years decided to oust them from leadership because of their strong stance on the inerrancy of the Bible. Then both her husband and father died. Grieving the loss of crucial relationships and getting a cancer diagnosis, Anne recognized it took immense Holy Spirit help and comfort and direction for her not to fall into a deep pit and never climb out. She writes with complete authenticity because experiencing the Holy Spirit is not just theory or doctrine to her, it's her lifeline!

Next up on my reading list was *It's Not Supposed to Be This Way: Finding Unexpected Strength When Disappointments Leave You Shattered* by Lysa TerKeurst. She honestly and humbly tells her story of being diagnosed with breast cancer right around the same time as her marriage imploded. Heartbreaking stuff! Lysa is a best-selling author and heads a huge ministry called Proverbs 31. She is a much-sought-after speaker and, of course, has a huge social media platform.

Adding pain to Lysa's trials were the horribly judgmental comments some made from a distance, actually blaming her for her husband's choices. The criticism was that a woman couldn't be successful in a big way and be a good wife at the same time; like, if you're going to be wildly popular, there's a price to pay. So she lost her husband (for a time), her breasts and health (health came back), and many so-called friends and supporters all at once. Oh the loneliness, the bleakness of those days for her. Yet God prompted her to write, to share, to give hope through her story to people like me, struggling through my own hard time. Whenever I was tempted to doubt God's love for me or His power over factors in my life, I'd think of all Lysa had been through and how she'd come out the other side with her faith intact and stronger than ever. Tragedy, darkness, triumph.

I read a biography called *Clara's War: One Girl's Story of Survival* by Clara Kramer, Kathy Kacer, and Stephen Glantz. It was a haunting true story of a young Jewish girl who hid with her family and fourteen others in a bunker beneath the house of the Polish man who rescued them. With straw laid down on the dirt for beds, their toilet was two buckets at one end of the bunker. Food—consisting mostly of potatoes—was handed down through a trapdoor. All the while, Nazi soldiers and SS men lived in the house above the bunker, so they couldn't make any noise at all. This lasted for eighteen months.

Now, why did this story comfort me? Well, at one point in the story, Clara got a rash all over her body due to bedbugs and lice from the dirty straw she was sleeping on. Someone had lowered down a bucket of apples instead of the usual potatoes. They tasted so delicious but gave her horrible diarrhea. I could only imagine what it was like sleeping on filthy, slimy straw and tiptoeing to a bucket to be sick in with fourteen other people in hearing distance and not having any access to medicine—all while experiencing the anxiety of possibly being discovered and shot.

The comfort part? I'm getting there. I was put on a new chemo drug and promptly developed horrible diarrhea and a rash on my inner thigh and couldn't keep food down. My doctor advised me to ride the symptoms out. But the symptoms continued for two weeks straight, and by week three I was so weak and lethargic that he admitted me to the hospital to uncover what was going on. He insisted it could not be the new chemo, that there was something else wrong. One of the tests involved me drinking liters of this liquid so they could do a scan. Well, in my condition, all that liquid had to come out . . . all night long. Up and down seventeen times, and yes, I counted. But because my mind was full of Clara's story and all she'd been through, I could only thank God that this little sickness was all I had to deal with. I kept saying, *Thank you, God, for clean sheets, toilets that flush, doctors and medicine to attend my ills, and freedom! You are so good to me, and I will praise You!*

Dwelling on the horrors that someone else went through as they experienced symptoms similar to mine made me less prone to self-pity. And thinking of the beautiful ways God saved and miraculously healed this whole Jewish family through such dire circumstances gave me hope and courage to carry on in dealing with my own sickness with a joyful attitude and the hope of complete rescue. Such comfort!

But the books that helped me the most through the worst of times, over a long period, were the four books of the series called *Sensible Shoes* by Sharon Garlough Brown. It's like God wrote them exactly for me for such a time as this.

The way the books came to me reassured me they were heaven-sent right from the start. I got a message from a lovely young gal named Ashley, who went to our church and had been in a class I'd taught there. She'd heard through the grapevine about my cancer diagnosis and felt compelled to tell me about these books. I ordered the first one and read it cover to cover in a couple of days, then messaged her back with great thanks for the recommendation. There were study guides to go along with the books and my new friend thought it would helpful to gather a community of women to read all the books together and discuss them. She set up a WhatsApp group for all of us, and throughout most of the long months of my cancer treatments, we corresponded.

The combination of spiritual wisdom from the books, which follow the fictional lives of four women going through various trials and the real-life application of the experiences each of us in the group was going through was powerful. The women in the books, Hannah, Meg, Charrisa, and Mara, each had issues that I was currently dealing with.

Hannah had worked at a church for fifteen years and had been forced to take a nine-month sabbatical against her will. She hated it. She was good at her job and loved helping others. She did not know who she was apart from her role as a pastor. I'd worked at our church for exactly fifteen years and still felt a bit adrift from not being able to be involved with ministry like I used to be. I could give but had a very hard time receiving. I loved having quick and fast spiritual answers for everyone, but how deep did they penetrate my own brokenness? Hannah and I were both told to "just rest" for at least nine months. That's a gestation period! What would the Lord birth anew in her, in me? (I do know she's fictional! But I felt like she was real.)

Meg had an only daughter whom she loved with all her heart who had pulled away from her emotionally and spiritually because she was involved in a sexual relationship with someone that Meg sensed would hurt her. My precious daughter Molly was in a relationship with another woman that I knew would not enhance her life in any way. I sensed anguish in Moll's soul and a fracture between her and God. Like Meg, I had very little power to head off what looked like a disaster waiting to befall my child.

Mara struggled with deep insecurities stemming from a checkered past. She had relational issues as she sought to please everyone around her. Loneliness embodied her at times. I knew God was calling out my own superficiality in relationships. The thinking that if I could just keep myself hidden enough by being pleasant to all, maybe I'd be accepted by all, was skewed and had to be undone.

Charissa dealt with pride issues and a performance-based self-worth that was off the charts. At one point she is bedridden with a risky pregnancy and her comments and thoughts of uselessness matched mine so completely as I lay in my own bed, it was almost eerie. Her overdeveloped sense of responsibility to excel struck a chord with me too.

I saw bits of myself in every character. The hope, the help, the healing that came to these women through the spiritual direction of a counselor named Katherine in the stories came very clearly and loudly to me. The novelty of reading fiction that was coupled with instruction in and examples of different spiritual practices that can help you connect with God in fresh ways was what made these books stand out. The story line was compelling and kept you reading, but the study guide made you take note of Scriptures and practices the characters used to move forward into more freedom and, of course, directly challenged you to apply them to your own life.

The women I was gathering with over WhatsApp were so amazing and diverse. Many of them lived in Niger, Africa, as missionaries, each originally from different countries or states within the US. Some were young moms, some more middle-aged, and a couple were empty-nesters like me. One gal, Joy (which was such an appropriate name for this amazing woman), had been through breast cancer, so she knew my current struggles. One gal was a chaplain's wife and they were still on active duty with the army, so she fully understood my life of moving around a lot. Another struggled with anxiety, so my fears were relatable to her. One had been through multiple miscarriages while working as a midwife and helping others continually have their own babies. Another had unexplained health issues that forced her off the mission field and back to England for laborious tests. There were deaths of loved ones among us, elderly parents falling ill and needing serious long-term care, children walking away from God in big ways, others just not thriving. I mention all this because our little group was truly going through all the trials and tribulations the world has to offer, yet together we were determined to grow in our faith, determined to take heart because Jesus was our Overcomer.

We were challenged by Sharon Garlough Brown, through her "true to life" characters, to find some real healing for the inner struggles and brokenness we all live with through true spiritual connection to the One who heals. We challenged each other to persevere, to think differently, to open up more to the love of Jesus. At the end of our journey together, we contacted Sharon, the author, and she graciously met with us over Zoom (not an easy task considering we were dealing with five different time zones!). She gave us insight into her creation of these characters. It was the capstone on all these months of learning and growing together. I'm actually going to start the series all over next month with a new group of women.

Words—through books, through the voices of friends and family and podcast guests—were used mightily by my Creator to show Himself to me. Community—His Spirit in others touching the Spirit in me was where I consistently found hope during the worst of this last season. God was with me every step of the way, loving me in exactly the ways I needed because He knows me best and loves me best. He made me a reader, a listener so when I'm letting words in, pondering the meanings, chewing on the ideas, I feel His pleasure.

EPILOGUE

Knowing All Will Be Well;
Every Manner of Thing
Will Be Well

I was under the impression that after six months of chemo, two operations, and six weeks of daily radiation, my cancer treatments would be over, but my oncologist decided it would be wise for me to take six more months of a preventative type of chemo in order to increase the chances that the cancer would not return. He predicted that the side effects would be minimal and I could return, somewhat, to normal life. I had all these glorious plans: trips to California to see two of my sons and their families; a couple of speaking engagements; a road trip with the podcast team; a huge family reunion; a cruise of New England and Canada with my prayer group friends and our hubbies to celebrate my birthday and being done with treatments; and other such fabulous adventures.

And then COVID-19 swept our world and everything shut down for a time. It was so bizarre. Our podcast team was going to be helping with a big women's conference being held in our area. We had hotel reservations and plans to meet exciting people, like Laura Story, who was leading worship for the event (I couldn't wait to tell her how much her book and songs had encouraged me) and Jennifer Rothschild, the main speaker, whom we'd interviewed on our podcast and fallen in love with. Her story was another one that gave me a picture of resilience through tragedy. She went blind as a teenager, yet through God's help and the hope she had in His love and grace and purpose, she's led an extremely fruitful, influential life.

The night before we were to leave for the conference, the NCAA canceled March Madness. What? Is this thing that serious? Apparently yes, as our conference was canceled too. We all were being urged to stay home. All my trips had to be canceled. No California, no cruise, not even church or coffee klatches in the neighborhood. Our pool and gym closed. I'd just spent ten months of my life somewhat isolated, and now it looked like I'd be staying home some more. Oh, the woe!

But when both the devotional I was reading and the podcast I was listening to quoted the very same story, I knew God had a point to drive home to me. It was about Julian of Norwich, who was an anchoress (meaning she made it her life purpose to withdraw from society and pray, kind of like a monk). Julian lived in England during the bubonic plague, which killed one-third of all Europeans. She became sick herself at one point. Thinking she was dying, she had a clear vision from the Lord. He said to her, "All will be well, all will be well, and every manner of thing will be well."[1] She lived two more decades. Hearing this story—twice, mind you—gave me incredible peace. I'd like to stay here two more decades, even though I hear heaven is a great place to be!

I read a book that mentioned a powerful study done on a group of people who had been traumatized in various ways yet did not develop PTSD; instead they actually experienced post-traumatic growth. Authors Jay and Katherine Wolf, of the book *Suffer Strong: How to Survive Anything by Redefining Everything*, write about the real possibility of growing stronger, better, more like Jesus as we suffer trauma and come through it with faith.

According to the study, these people had five things in common. They:

- Felt a renewed appreciation for life
- Saw new possibilities for themselves
- Felt more personal strength
- Saw their relationships improved
- Felt more spiritually satisfied[2]

As I read that list, I was comforted that all five are true in my own life. I'll explain how, but I want to make it very clear that I'm not saying this in a boastful, bragging way! All glory goes to God and His Spirit within me working like only He can to help a person grow despite circumstances.

A Renewed Appreciation for Life

Before my ten months of seclusion due to chemotherapy, surgery, and radiation, I enjoyed life but didn't deeply appreciate the little things. Thankfully, I had a couple of months of normalcy between the end of those treatments and the start of the COVID shutdowns. I cannot tell you how much I appreciated being able to drive again, hug people, shop, take long walks with my husband, attend church, and a whole host of activities that I'd really just taken for granted. Everything sparkled. Rejoice in the Lord, always! Then the pandemic hit and the new chemo I started actually did have side effects. Would I still appreciate life?

New Possibilities

Yes, I could rejoice, because I clearly saw a new possibility. I've always wanted to write a book, but I could never sit still long enough to actually do it. I realized that this new season of life would be the perfect time to make that dream come true. I'm writing now and the hope that I could actually produce a book is bringing me great joy.

More Personal Strength

Although my body is weak, I feel like my inner self is stronger. I have more self-knowledge. I have been weaned of thinking that productivity equals value, that busyness equals importance. I'm able to find my identity in Christ alone. One of my favorite verses now is 2 Corinthians 4:16: "Therefore, we do not lose heart, but though our outer man is decaying, our inner man is being renewed day by day."

Improved Relationships

I've always loved my three brothers and my sister, but we live far from each other. We had intense family reunions, but only once or twice a year. Between these reunions, we had little contact with each other because of our busyness.

My sister has come from California and stayed with me four different times this past year. My brothers and their wives have visited several times. We have a weekly bridge club and family get-togethers on Zoom now. I've never felt closer to them. I feel like they really know me for who I am now and vice versa. My precious daughter stayed with me for weeks at a time during the worst of the chemo and surgery. All three of my sons came with their wives and babies and helped me. My husband has been a treasure, literally doing everything around the house. My heart truly bursts with more love for my family.

My podcast teammates and listening audience, my prayer group friends, my home-group people—even my new neighbors—all have an incredibly deeper place in my heart now, than ever before. One guy in my home group, whom Mike and I have always been close with, hugged me so tight the first time I saw him after the diagnosis that he communicated love and care for me without using words. It brought tears to my eyes and to this day I know we will be friends forever. I feel so raw and open with people now and I think that deepens relationships.

More Spiritually Satisfied

I told you about one of our first podcast guests, Donna Tyson, who talked about her journey with breast cancer, saying that she wouldn't trade what she'd been through—even though parts of it were awful—because she had a new intimacy with Jesus that was priceless. I wondered about that until I experienced it myself.

Jesus told us all very bluntly that in this world we would have trouble. But then He urged us all to "take heart" because He had overcome the world. We all get the trouble part. I've laid out all my personal woes from the very petty (ruined vacations) to the more serious (death of loved ones and facing my own possible death) and everything in between. As I'm writing, we as a nation have gone through race riots and political unrest and economic downturns, it's been a full year since COVID-19 hit, and we are still wearing masks and social distancing. Trouble with a capital T, personally and globally. It's a hard world. But exactly how do we "take heart"? By putting our faith in the One who overcomes it all; by finding our hope in God, the Hope Giver; by finding our help in Jesus, who died on the cross to save us; by finding our healing in the Spirit, who was sent to comfort us and teach us and bring wholeness.

I spoke parts of my story here simply to show that God is real and He cared enough about me to send *hope* when I needed life to be bigger than it was, when I needed to feel suffering could be productive and not ruin me, when I needed to be lifted from self-pity.

He sent *help* when I needed to lead but no one wanted to follow, when I was over my head in ministry responsibilities, when I had relational issues with my husband and parenting issues with my kids, when I had fractured friendships.

And He sent *healing* when I was cancer-ridden, when the brokenness of my past threatened to undo my future, when my theology needed repair, and when my self-image needed an infusion of His truth.

Seek Him and you will find Him to be enough in this hard world. Then call me up and share your story with me! Stories change lives and I want to thank you, dear reader, for spending time absorbing mine. I hope (there's that word again!) it has helped (I can't stop with the H words!) and that your future will include all kinds of action steps like pondering and searching and receiving and knowing Truth. When we actively walk with Him, this hard world doesn't seem so awful, just full of opportunities to watch Him shine in us and through us.

I leave you with words from the book of Daniel: "Men and women who have lived wisely and well will shine brilliantly, like the cloudless, star-strewn night skies. And those who put others on the right path to life will glow like stars forever" (Daniel 12:3, MSG). Let's all speak our stories to help one another live wisely and well and find the path that connects to the great love of God.

ENDNOTES

Prologue: Addressing a Broken Heart

1. Casey Cep, *Furious Hours: Murder, Fraud, and the last trial of Harper Lee* (New York: Radom House, 2019), 324.

2. David G. Allen, TEDx Talk transcript: "Who Knows What's Good or Bad?" (September 1, 2015), first three paragraphs.

3. Brené Brown, *Rising Strong: How the Ability to Reset Transforms the Way We Live, Love, Parent, and Lead* (New York: Random House, 2015), 6.

Chapter 1: Pondering Thought-Jolting Conversations

1. Janet Flaherty, "Notable Nonsense" column in the *Milton Courier* (Milton, Wisconsin), Tom and Alice Flaherty, *Notable Nonsense Column Collection*, (Fosston, Minnesota. 1995) last page.

> Humble Origins
>
> I was reading a biography recently that went something like this: "Born and raised in a small town in the Midwest, John was the son of an itinerant printer and a schoolmarm. Leaving all this behind he climbed to fame and fortune."
>
> The implication seemed to be that his childhood was a severe handicap which should best be quickly forgotten. He had risen above that.
>
> It sounded reasonable at first until I realized that pompous biographer was describing someone like me. Then I was miffed. Imagine, after depleting one's purse, energies and nervous system, to be dismissed in one sentence. What, pray tell, is wrong with being

in a small town in the Midwest—except that most biographers live in New York and have no concept of the Midwest. They probably don't even know where Wisconsin is.

Just let one of my children become famous and write that nonsense and I'll haunt them forever. That "schoolmarm" title brings up visions of the matronly type, gray hair done up in a tight bun, rimless glasses and a stout ruler in hand. And "itinerant printer". . . well maybe Mike can live with that.

On second thought, if any biographies get written around here I'll do it myself: "Born of highly intelligent parents in a stimulating Midwest society and blessed with a particularly charming mother . . .

Chapter 2: Changing Worldviews

1. Josh and Sean McDowell, *More Than a Carpenter* (Carol Stream: Tyndale Momentum, 1977), 168.

Chapter 3: Seeking Healthiness: Body, Soul, and Spirit

1. C. S. Lewis, *The Problem of Pain,* quoted in *C. S. Lewis' Little Book of Wisdom: Meditations on Faith, Love, Life, and Literature* (Charlottesville, VA: Hampton Roads Publishing, 2018), 91.

2. Baltimore Catechism No. 1 (London: Baronius Press, 2006), 11.

Chapter 5: Searching for Truth

1. The saying "in essentials unity, in nonessentials liberty, in all things charity" is often attributed to Saint Augustine, but it really comes from an otherwise undistinguished German Lutheran theologian of the early seventeenth century, Rupertus Meldenius. The phrase occurs in a tract on Christian unity circa 1627, during the Thirty Years War (1618–1648), a bloody time in European history in which religious tensions played a significant role. "In Nonessentials, Liberty!" *Reasoning from the Scriptures,*

October 20, 2011. http://destroyingspeculations.blogspot. com/2011/10/in-non-essentials-liberty-romans-141-12.html.

Chapter 6: Acknowledging the Sovereign Hand of God

1. Pierre Teilhard de Chardin is probably the source of this quote. Teilhard de Chardin was a French philosopher, paleontologist, and Jesuit priest who thought deeply on the meaning of our existence and relationship with the Divine. Betsy Koelzer, *We Are Spiritual Beings Having a Human Experience* (the clearingnw. com, September 5, 2013), https://www.theclearingnw.com/ blog/spiritual-beings-having-a-human-experience.

Chapter 7: Rejoicing in Terrible, Wonderful Things

1. For information on the Myers-Briggs Personality Test, go to https://www.myersbriggs.org.

2. "Just a Closer Walk with Thee" was written by an anonymous lyricist and first appeared as a popular jazz hymn around 1940. It has been published in more than ninety-nine hymnals and recorded by many performers across different musical genres.

3. Freedom of Choice Act. Freedom of Choice Act–FactCheck.org.
    1. All hospitals, including Catholic hospitals will be required to perform abortions upon request.
    2. Partial birth abortions would be legal and have no limitations.
    3. All US tax payers would be funding abortions.
    4. Parental notification will no longer be required.

Chapter 9: Navigating a Foreign Land

1. David Slater, "I Cast All Your Cares upon Me."

Chapter 13: Working for Money but Not Exclusively

1. The first part of this quote is from Saint Augustine. Saint Augustine Quotes, *Brainy Quote-Famous Quotes* (Brainy Media,

2001). https://www.brainyquote.com. Angus Buchan says this with the additional sentence in the movie *Faith like Potatoes: The Story of a Farmer Who Risked Everything for God* (Affirm Films/ Sony Pictures Home Entertainment, 2006), based on the book by Angus Buchan, *Faith like Potatoes: The Story of a Farmer Who Risked Everything for God* (Oxford: Lion Hudson PLC, 2006).

Chapter 15: Running from Selfish Ambition

1. Thom S. Rainer and Eric Geiger, *Simple Church: Returning to God's Process for Making Disciples* (Nashville: B&H Publishing Group, 2011).

2. "Guidance," Alpha. https://www.alpha.org/

Chapter 16: Wanting His Will More than Mine (Kind Of!)

1. Doctor Alicia Britt Chole, *7 Day Devotional, Godprints, 7 Days of Discovery* (delivered via email to subscribers, author included).

2. Max Lucado, *The Story* (Grand Rapids: Zondervan, 2005), 46–47.

3. Sharon Glasgow. *She Speaks Stories* Podcast Episode #5 https://shespeaksstories.com/listen

4. Michele Husfelt. *She Speaks Stories* Podcast Episode #6 https://shespeaksstories.com/listen

5. Rebecca Lyons. *She Speaks Stories* Podcast Episode #7 https://shespeaksstories.com/listen

Chapter 17: Relying Heavily on God's Provision

1. Katie Davis Majors. *She Speaks Stories* Podcast Episode #19 https://shespeaksstories.com/listen

2. Irene Rollins. *She Speaks Stories* Podcast Episode #18 https://shespeaksstories.com/listen

3. Anna LeBaron. *She Speaks Stories* Podcast Episode #20 https://shespeaksstories.com/listen

4. Margi McCombs. *She Speaks Stories* Podcast Episode #15 https:// shespeaksstories.com/listen

5. Kim Hyland. *She Speaks Stories* Podcast Episode #11 https:// shespeaksstories.com/listen

6. Sharie King. *She Speaks Stories* Podcast Episode #16 https://she-speaksstories.com/listen

7. Jessica Honegger. *She Speaks Stories* Podcast Episode #17 https:// shespeaksstories.com/listen

Chapter 18: Living Loved

1. Sean Curran, Allen Swoope, and Natalie Sims, "Bigger Than I Thought."

2. Skye Jethani, *With. Reimagining the Way You Relate to God* (Nashville: Thomas Nelson, 2011), opening chapters.

3. Skye Jethani, *With. Reimagining the Way You Relate to God*, 101.

4. Author Unknown, "A Tandem Bike Ride with God," quoted in "A tandem ride with God," Sisters for Sunshine, Nov. 1, 2012. sistersforsunshine.wordpress.com/2012/11/01/a-tandem-ride-with-god/.

5. Jonathan David Helser, Joel Case, Brian Mark Johnson. "No Longer Slaves." (Bethel Music, 2015).

6. "The Drowning Man," *Truthbook*. https://truthbook.com/stories/funny-god/the-drowning-man.

Chapter 19: Chewing on Words of Wisdom

1. Ashleigh Burnette, *She Speaks Stories* podcast Episode #65. https://shespeaksstories.com/listen

2. Jane Marczewski, *She Speaks Stories* podcast Episode #112. https://shespeaksstories.com/listen

3. Dr. Alicia Britt Chole, *She Speaks Stories* podcast Episode #136. https://shespeaksstories.com/listen

4. Tiffany Johnson, *She Speaks Stories* podcast Episode #130. https://shespeaksstories.com/listen

5. Philip Yancey, *Disappointment with God: Three Questions No One Asks Out Loud* (Grand Rapids: Zondervan, 1992).

6. Philip Yancey, *Disappointment with God: Three Questions No One Asks Out Loud*, 231–232.

7. Philip Yancey, *Disappointment with God: Three Questions No One Asks Out Loud*, 236.

8. Laura Story, "Blessings."

Epilogue: Knowing All Will Be Well; Every Manner of Things Will Be Well

1. Dan Graves, *Article #31 Christian History Institute. "All Shall Be Well,"* (https://christianhistoryinstitute.org/incontext/article/julian.)

2. Katherine and Jay Wolf, *Suffer Strong: How to Survive Anything by Redefining Everything* (Grand Rapids: Zondervan, 2020), 73.

ACKNOWLEDGMENTS

My great thanks to all who have helped me accomplish writing this book will not be listed here in order of importance but in kind of a loose chronological order of how this feat came about. So my undying love and gratitude go out:

To my brother, Tom, who first shared the gospel with me clearly and fearlessly and helped start a fire in me to even want to testify of the goodness of God.

To Susan Wanderer, for inviting me to start a podcast with her and being such a delightfully fun ministry partner to dream and scheme with, along with our whole She Speaks Story Team of Portia Allen, Gwen Curtis, and so many other lovely volunteers that help each week.

To Susan Blount, who was the first to champion our podcast and at one point mentioned, "Your next step is to write a book." She graciously steered us to an online teaching on how to write a book proposal. Then she spent precious time with me on the phone coaching me to think through what the book might look like. She's brilliant!

To Molly, my precious daughter, who couldn't believe someone mentioned I should write a book, because Molly and I talked about writing one together for years. But really we just talked about going on a book tour together and getting rich and famous because the book would be good. The problem always came down to "too bad we don't have anything to write about or have a clue how to write a book." She enthuses daily over whatever project I'm involved in and encourages me no end.

To Mike, and Matt and Jill, and John and Kelsey, my other fabulous children, who not only said they believed in the podcast but put their money where their mouths were and became generous donors. They asked often how the book was going and actually cared about the answer. They also produced the most adorable grandkids in the world—Connor, Lily, Thomas, Hunter, and Evie Jo—which gave me the incentive to leave a written legacy of God's exploits in my life so when I'm gone and they are running the world, they'll know all about Him from my point of view.

To the incredible *She Speaks Stories* community who cheered me on through cancer, prayed for me, sent me delightful messages despite me not answering with any clarity, and finally started encouraging me on this book-writing journey. So many said they'd actually read it if I ever finished it, so I did! I wish I had space to name names, but so many incredibly loving people are out there!

To my brothers and sisters (the biological ones, not the church ones) Mike and Diane, Bob and Denny, Tom and Alice, Jim and Angela, for caring about the written word, setting high standards in their own writings, encouraging me to keep at it, and loving me so well. The weekly phone calls and bridge club on Zoom helped me stay sane. Joyce and Charlie, nieces and nephews, Flaherty and Leahy, relatives, all added in their own ways a note here and there, a visit, an encouraging text or email, and every bit of those loving gestures spurred me on.

To God the Father, Jesus my Lord and Savior (see why I said not listed in order of importance!), who actually gave me something to write about and then gave me a couple of years of solitude to get it written. No one is really thankful for trials in this life, but in my case (since the biggies are over for now) I'm filled with gratitude to Him who walked with me intimately filling me with His Spirit. He really is my all in all.

To Lori Pikkaart, a friend and editor who painstakingly edited the very raw rough draft and wouldn't accept anything for it except some lunches out. She is so smart and gracious and talented that she truly saved me from writing foolishness, and I'm eternally grateful.

To Jennifer Edwards, a professional editor who graciously tackled the book next and gave me all kinds of wisdom to make it better, along with becoming a new friend. Then she introduced me to Athena Dean Holtz, founder and publisher of Redemption Press, who made me feel welcome and comfortable right off the bat. Her team of editors and project managers and designers were outstanding, and I'm so grateful to each for their contributions.

To the prayer team and the Holy Spirit who so fills each of them to the fullest. Prayer is the greatest work of all! It moves mountains, and all these friends have powerfully uttered words to God on behalf of this story. I wanted to list every name here, but the list got long, and I feared I'd leave someone out. I am truly grateful to this good-looking army of prayer warriors!

To Julia Sifers, captain of the hardworking launch team, and so much more to me personally. She truly is a daughter in Christ, a friend, a cheerleader, a fearless leader, and an excellent writer. To all the launch team members, who did an incredible job of getting the word out there!

To Therisa Bennett for the lovely artwork. She graces this world with so much beauty through her smile and friendship and her artistic abilities. She made this book so much better.

To my handsome husband. Now, I said this wasn't in order of

importance, and I meant it because the one person who swooped in and truly made this book happen was Mike. About halfway through the writing, I got discouraged and gave up. It all seemed dull and pointless. He breathed new energy into me, believed I really could write something interesting, and most of all financed the whole thing with hard-earned money because he knew if I had professionals helping me and deadlines to meet, I'd get it done. He encouraged me every step of the way and even let me tell some of the less flattering parts of our story together. He's a generous, gracious, and godly man, and I'm ever grateful he's mine.